Houghton
Mifflin
Harcourt

P9-CBB-325

CALIFORNIA
MATH
Expressions
Common Core

Dr. Karen C. Fuson

GRADE

3

Volume 2

This material is based upon work supported by the
National Science Foundation
under Grant Numbers
ESI-9816320, REC-9806020, and RED-935373.

Any opinions, findings, and conclusions, or recommendations expressed in this material
are those of the author and do not necessarily reflect the views of the National Science Foundation.

Printed in the U.S.A.

ISBN: 978-0-544-21082-0

14 15 16 0868 23 22 21

4500819730   B C D E F G

VOLUME 2 CONTENTS

UNIT 4 Multidigit Addition and Subtraction

UNIT 5 Write Equations to Solve Word Problems

© Houghton Mifflin Harcourt Publishing Company

UNIT 6 Polygons, Perimeter, and Area

BIG IDEA 1	Analyzing Triangles and Quadrilaterals

BIG IDEA 2	Area and Perimeter

© Houghton Mifflin Harcourt Publishing Company

UNIT 7 Explore Fractions

Family Letter

Content Overview

Dear Family,

Your child is currently participating in math activities that help him or her to understand place value, rounding, and addition and subtraction of 3-digit numbers.

- **Place Value Drawings:** Students learn to represent numbers with drawings that show how many hundreds, tens, and ones are in the numbers. Hundreds are represented by boxes. Tens are represented by vertical line segments, called ten sticks. Ones are represented by small circles. The drawings are also used to help students understand regrouping in addition and subtraction. Here is a place value drawing for the number 178.

| 1 hundred | 7 tens | 8 ones |

The 7 ten sticks and 8 circles are grouped in 5s so students can see the quantities easily and avoid errors.

- **Secret Code Cards:** Secret Code Cards are a set of cards for hundreds, tens, and ones. Students learn about place value by assembling the cards to show two- and three-digit numbers. Here is how the number 148 would be assembled.

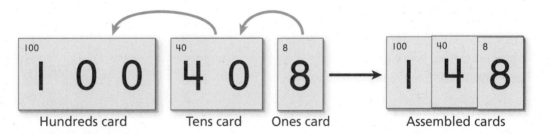

Hundreds card   Tens card   Ones card   Assembled cards

Estimate Sums and Differences Students learn to estimate sums and differences by rounding numbers. They also use estimates to check that their actual answers are reasonable.

	Rounded to the nearest hundred	Rounded to the nearest ten
493	500	490
129	100	130
+ 369	+ 400	+ 370
991	Estimate: 1,000	Estimate: 990

Make Place Value Drawings **223**

Family Letter

Content Overview

Addition Methods: Students may use the common U.S. method, referred to as the New Groups Above Method, as well as two alternative methods. In the New Groups Below Method, students add from right to left and write the new ten and new hundred on the line. In the Show All Totals method, students add in either direction, write partial sums and then add the partial sums to get the total. Students also use proof drawings to demonstrate grouping 10 ones to make a new ten and grouping 10 tens to make a new hundred.

The New Groups Below Method shows the teen number 13 better than does the New Groups Above Method, where the 1 and 3 are separated. Also, addition is easier in New Groups Below, where you add the two numbers you see and just add 1.

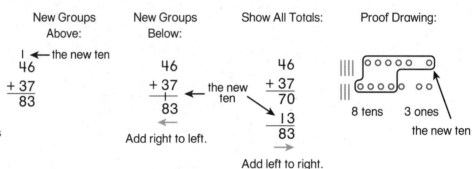

New Groups Above:

```
 1  ← the new ten
 46
+37
 83
```

New Groups Below:

```
  46
+ 37
  1
  83
```
← the new ten

Add right to left.

Show All Totals:

```
  46
+ 37
  70
  13
  83
```

Add left to right.

Proof Drawing:

8 tens   3 ones
the new ten

Subtraction Methods: Students may use the common U.S. method in which the subtraction is done right to left, with the ungrouping done before each column is subtracted. They also learn an alternative method in which all the ungrouping is done *before* the subtracting. If they do all the ungrouping first, students can subtract either from left to right or from right to left.

The Ungroup First Method helps students avoid the common error of subtracting a smaller top number from a larger bottom number.

1. Ungroup first
2. Subtract (from left to right or from right to left).

```
    15
  3 513
  463
- 275
  188
```

Ungroup 1 hundred to make 10 tens.

Ungroup 1 ten to make 10 ones.

3 hundreds   15 tens   13 ones

Please call if you have any questions or comments.

Thank you.

Sincerely,
Your child's teacher

CA CC

Unit 4 addresses the following standards from the *Common Core State Standards for Mathematics with California Additions*: **3.OA.8, 3.NBT.1, 3.NBT.2,** and all Mathematical Practices.

© Houghton Mifflin Harcourt Publishing Company

Make Place Value Drawings

Carta a la familia

Un vistazo general al contenido

Estimada familia:

Su niño está participando en actividades matemáticas que le servirán para comprender el valor posicional, el redondeo y la suma y resta de números de 3 dígitos.

- **Dibujos de valor posicional:** Los estudiantes aprenden a representar números por medio de dibujos que muestran cuántas centenas, decenas y unidades contienen. Las centenas están representadas con casillas, las decenas con segmentos verticales, llamados palitos de decenas, y las unidades con círculos pequeños. Los dibujos también se usan para ayudar a los estudiantes a comprender cómo se reagrupa en la suma y en la resta. Este es un dibujo de valor posicional para el número 178.

1 centena   7 decenas   8 unidades

Los palitos de decenas y los círculos se agrupan en grupos de 5 para que las cantidades se puedan ver más fácilmente y se eviten errores.

- **Tarjetas de código secreto:** Las tarjetas de código secreto son un conjunto de tarjetas con centenas, decenas y unidades. Los estudiantes aprenden acerca del valor posicional organizando las tarjetas de manera que muestren números de dos y de tres dígitos. Así se puede formar el número 148:

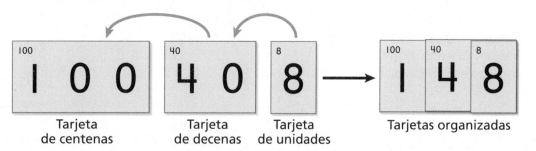

Tarjeta de centenas   Tarjeta de decenas   Tarjeta de unidades   Tarjetas organizadas

Estimar sumas y diferencias: Los estudiantes aprenden a estimar sumas y diferencias redondeando números. También usan las estimaciones para comprobar que sus respuestas son razonables.

		Redondear a la centena más próxima		Redondear a la decena más próxima
	493	500		490
	129	100		130
	+ 369	+ 400		+ 370
	991	Estimación: 1,000		Estimación: 990

Carta a la familia

Un vistazo general al contenido

Métodos de suma: Los estudiantes pueden usar el método común de EE. UU., conocido como Grupos nuevos arriba, y otros dos métodos alternativos. En el método de Grupos nuevos abajo, los estudiantes suman de derecha a izquierda y escriben la nueva decena y la nueva centena en el renglón. En el método de Mostrar todos los totales, los estudiantes suman en cualquier dirección, escriben sumas parciales y luego las suman para obtener el total. Los estudiantes también usan dibujos de comprobación para demostrar cómo se agrupan 10 unidades para formar una nueva decena, y 10 decenas para formar una nueva centena.

El método de Grupos nuevos abajo muestra el número 13 mejor que el método de Grupos nuevos arriba, en el que se separan los números 1 y 3. Además, es más fácil sumar con Grupos nuevos abajo, donde se suman los dos números que se ven y simplemente se añade 1.

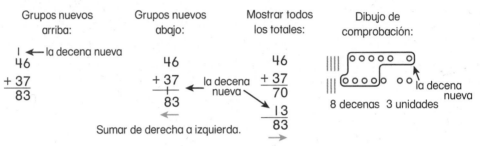

Grupos nuevos arriba:

1 ← la decena nueva
46
+ 37
83

Grupos nuevos abajo:

46
+ 37
83   ← la decena nueva

Sumar de derecha a izquierda.

Mostrar todos los totales:

46
+ 37
70
13
83

Sumar de izquierda a derecha.

Dibujo de comprobación:

8 decenas   3 unidades   la decena nueva

Métodos de resta: Los estudiantes pueden usar el método común de EE. UU., en el cual la resta se hace de derecha a izquierda, desagrupando antes de restar cada columna. También aprenden un método alternativo en el que desagrupan todo *antes* de restar. Si los estudiantes desagrupan todo primero, pueden restar de izquierda a derecha o de derecha a izquierda.

El método de Desagrupar primero ayuda a los estudiantes a evitar el error común de restar un número pequeño de arriba, de un número más grande de abajo.

1. Desagrupar primero.
2. Restar (de izquierda a derecha o de derecha a izquierda).

15
3 5 13
4̶6̶3̶
− 275
188

Desagrupar 1 centena para formar 10 decenas.   Desagrupar 1 decena para formar 10 unidades.

3 centenas   15 decenas   13 unidades

Si tiene alguna pregunta o algún comentario, por favor comuníquese conmigo. Gracias.

Atentamente,
El maestro de su niño

CA CC

En la Unidad 4 se aplican los siguientes estándares auxiliares, contenidos en los *Estándares estatales comunes de matemáticas con adiciones para California:* **3.OA.8, 3.NBT.1, 3.NBT.2,** y todos los de prácticas matemáticas.

© Houghton Mifflin Harcourt Publishing Company

226 UNIT 4 LESSON 1

Make Place Value Drawings

CA CC Content Standards 3.NBT.1, 3.NBT.2
Mathematical Practices MP.2

Name _____ **Date** _____

► Practice Place Value Drawings to 999

Write the number for each dot drawing.

1.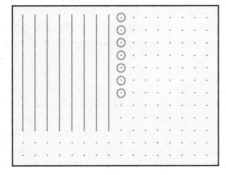

2.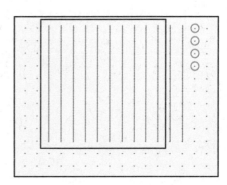

_____   _____

Write the number for each place value drawing.

3. □ □ ||||| || ⦾⦾⦾⦾⦾ ⦾⦾

_____

4. □ □ □ ||||| | ⦾

_____

5. □ □ □ || ⦾⦾⦾
   □ □ □

_____

6. □ □ □ |||| ⦾⦾⦾⦾⦾ ⦾⦾⦾⦾
   □

_____

Make a place value drawing for each number.

7. 86

8. 587

▶ Practice with the Thousand Model

Write the number for each place value drawing.

9.

10.

_____   _____

Make a place value drawing for each number.

11. 2,368

12. 5,017

▶ Write Numbers for Word Names

Write the number for the words.

13. eighty-two _____

14. ninety-nine _____

15. four hundred sixty-seven _____

16. nine hundred six _____

17. one thousand, fifteen _____

18. eight thousand, one hundred twenty _____

1	2	10	20
1	2	1 0	2 0

3	4	30	40
3	4	3 0	4 0

5	6	50	60
5	6	5 0	6 0

7	8	70	80
7	8	7 0	8 0

9	90	100
9	9 0	1 0 0

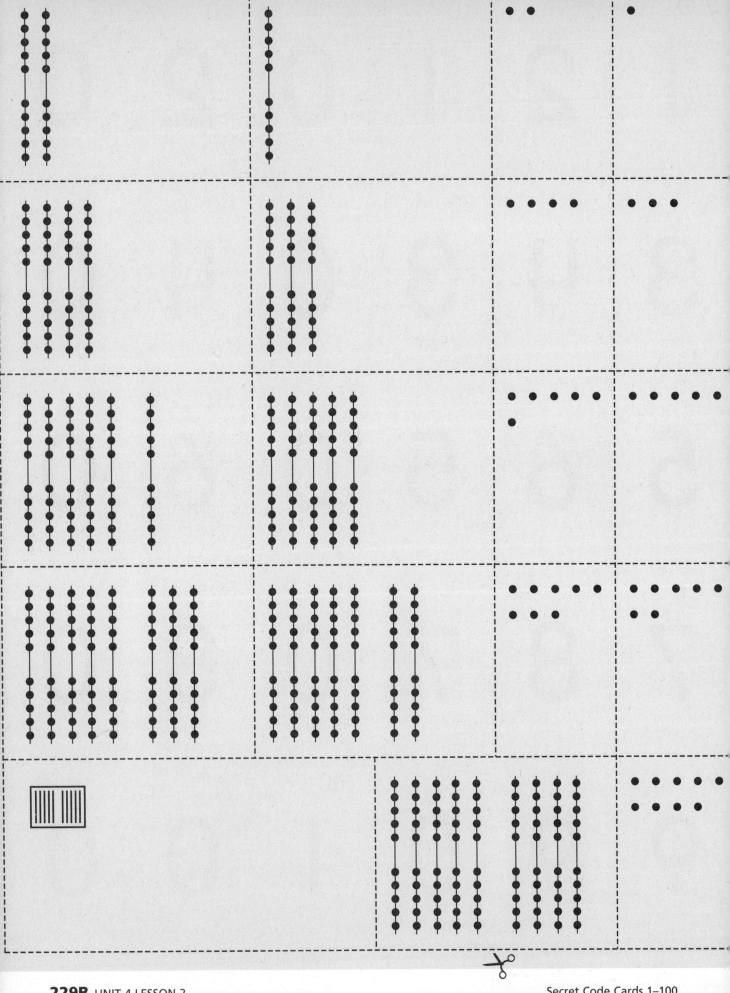

Secret Code Cards 1–100

200
2 0 0

300
3 0 0

400
4 0 0

500
5 0 0

600
6 0 0

700
7 0 0

800
8 0 0

900
9 0 0

1000
1 0 0 0

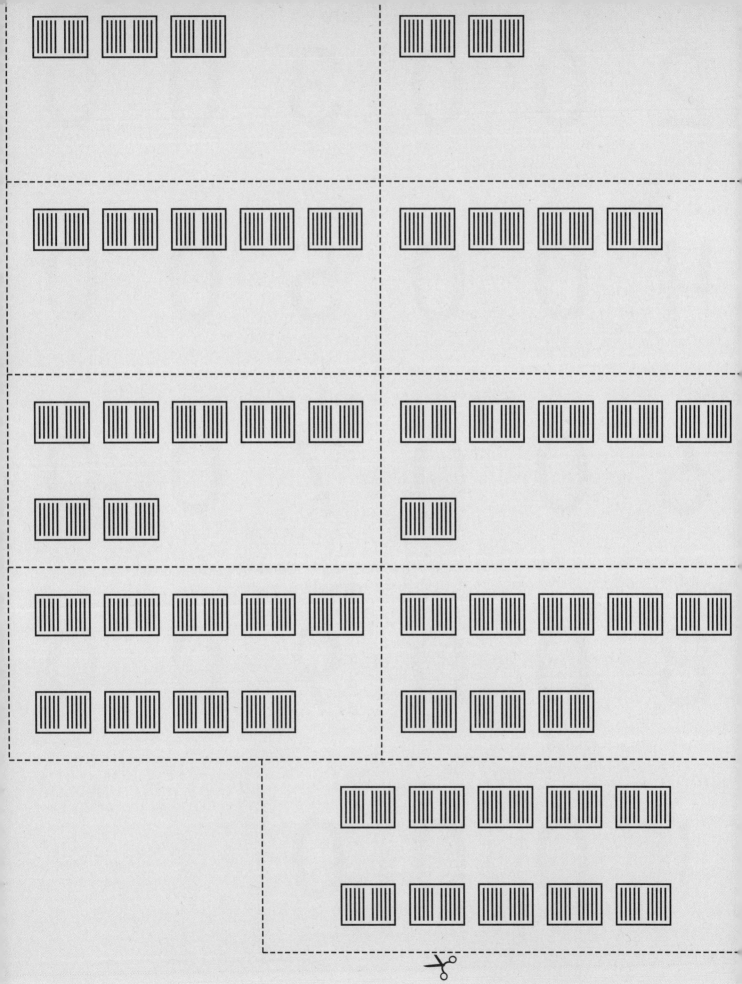

Name _____ **Date** _____

CA CC Content Standards 3.NBT.1, 3.NBT.2
Mathematical Practices MP.1, MP.4, MP.7

> **VOCABULARY**
> expanded form
> standard form

▶ Read and Write Numbers

Write the number for the words.

1. two hundred twelve _____

2. two thousand, eight _____

3. nine hundred ninety-one _____

4. six thousand, fifty-one _____

5. four hundred sixteen _____

6. six hundred nine _____

7. nine hundred eighty-seven

_____

8. five thousand, thirty

_____

9. four thousand, seventeen

_____

10. eight thousand, six hundred

_____

Write the word name for each number.

11. 783

_____

12. 907

_____

13. 3,001

_____

14. 8,043

_____

Write each number in expanded form.

15. 314 _____

16. 2,148 _____

17. 7,089 _____

18. 8,305 _____

Write each number in standard form.

19. 5 thousands + 8 tens + 7 ones

_____

20. 6 thousands + 4 hundreds + 5 ones

_____

► **Solve and Discuss**

Use a place value drawing to help you solve each
problem. Label your answers.

Show your work.

21. Scott baked a batch of rolls. He gave a bag of
    10 rolls to each of 7 friends. He kept 1 roll
    for himself. How many rolls did he bake in all?

    _____

22. Sixty-two bags of hot dog buns were delivered to
    the school cafeteria. Each bag had 10 buns. How
    many buns were delivered?

    _____

Mario and Rosa baked 89 corn muffins.
They put the muffins in boxes of 10.

---

23. How many boxes did they fill?   24. How many muffins were left
                                                over?

    _____   _____

Zoe's scout troop collected 743 cans of food to
donate to a shelter. They put the cans in boxes
of 10.

---

25. How many boxes did they fill?   26. How many cans were left over?

    _____   _____

27. **Math Journal** Write your own place value word
    problem. Make a drawing to show how to solve
    your problem.

CA CC Content Standards 3.NBT.1, 3.NBT.2
Mathematical Practices MP.1, MP.7

► Scrambled Place Value Names

Unscramble the place values and write the number.

1. 8 **ones** + 6 **hundreds** + 4 **tens**

   _____

2. 9 hundreds + 7 tens + 1 one

   _____

3. 5 ones + 0 tens + 7 hundreds

   _____

4. 5 tens + 4 ones + 3 hundreds

   _____

5. 2 tens + 2 hundreds + 2 ones

   _____

6. 8 hundreds + 3 ones + 6 tens

   _____

Unscramble the place values and write the number.
Then, make a place value drawing for the number.

7. 6 hundreds + 9 ones + 3 tens

   _____

8. 9 ones + 3 tens + 8 hundreds

   _____

9. 8 ones + 3 hundreds + 4 tens

   _____

10. 2 hundreds + 9 tens + 1 one

   _____

▶ Solve and Discuss

Solve each problem. Label your answer.

11. The bookstore received 35 boxes of books.
Each box held 10 books. How many books did
the store receive?

_____

Maya's family picked 376 apples and put them
in baskets. Each basket held 10 apples.

12. How many baskets did they fill?   13. How many apples were left over?

_____   _____

Aidee had 672 buttons. She put them in bags
of 100 buttons each.

14. How many bags did Aidee fill?   15. How many buttons were left over?

_____   _____

When Joseph broke open his piggy bank, there
were 543 pennies inside. He grouped the pennies
into piles of 100.

16. How many piles of 100 did   17. How many extra pennies did he
Joseph make?   have?

_____   _____

Practice with Place Value

Name _____ **Date** _____

CA CC Content Standards 3.NBT.1, 3.NBT.2
Mathematical Practices MP.1, MP.2, MP.8

► Estimate

Solve the problem.

1. Tasha read three books over the summer. Here is the number of pages in each book:

Watership Down	494 pages
Sounder	128 pages
The Secret Garden	368 pages

   About how many pages did Tasha read? Explain how you made your **estimate**.

   _____

   _____

► Practice Rounding

Round each number to the nearest hundred. Use drawings or Secret Code Cards if they help you.

2. 128 _____   3. 271 _____   4. 376 _____

5. 649 _____   6. 415 _____   7. 550 _____

8. 62 _____   9. 1,481 _____   10. 2,615 _____

11. **Explain Your Thinking** When you round a number to the nearest hundred, how do you know whether to round up or round down?

   _____

   _____

   _____

   _____

► **Solve Problems by Estimating**

Solve by rounding to the nearest hundred.   *Show your work.*

12. At the Lakeside School, there are 286 second graders, 341 third graders, and 377 fourth graders. About how many students are there at the Lakeside School?

_____

13. Last week, Mrs. Larson drove 191 miles on Monday, 225 miles on Wednesday, and 107 miles on Friday. About how many miles did she drive altogether?

_____

14. Of the 832 people at the hockey game, 292 sat on the visiting team side. The rest sat on the home team side. About how many people sat on the home team side?

_____

► **Reasonable Answers**

Use rounding to decide if the answer is reasonable. Then find the answer to see if you were right.

15. $604 - 180 = 586$

_____

17. $268 - 17 = 107$

_____

19. $407 - 379 = 28$

_____

16. $377 + 191 = 568$

_____

18. $1{,}041 + 395 = 646$

_____

20. $535 + 287 = 642$

_____

CA CC Content Standards 3.NBT.1, 3.NBT.2
Mathematical Practices MP.1, MP.2, MP.3, MP.6, MP.8

Name _____ **Date** _____

▶ Round 2-Digit Numbers to the Nearest Ten

Round each number to the nearest ten.

1. 63 _____

2. 34 _____

3. 78 _____

4. 25 _____

5. 57 _____

6. 89 _____

7. 42 _____

8. 92 _____

▶ Round 3-Digit Numbers to the Nearest Ten

Round each number to the nearest ten.

9. 162 _____

10. 741 _____

11. 309 _____

12. 255 _____

13. 118 _____

14. 197 _____

15. 503 _____

16. 246 _____

17. **Explain Your Thinking** When you round a number to the nearest ten, how do you know whether to round up or round down?

_____

_____

_____

_____

▶ Estimate the Answer

Solve each problem.

18. The chart at the right shows how many smoothies the Juice Hut sold yesterday. By rounding each number to the nearest ten, estimate how many smoothies the Juice Hut sold in all.

Smoothies Sold at Juice Hut
13 raspberry-peach smoothies
38 strawberry-banana smoothies
44 guava-mango smoothies
61 peach-blueberry smoothies

19. Ms. Singh has 52 rock CDs, 75 jazz CDs, 36 classical CDs, and 23 hip-hop CDs. Round each number to the nearest ten to find *about* how many CDs she has.

20. Roz rented a video that is 123 minutes long. She watched 48 minutes of it. Round each number to the nearest ten to estimate how many more minutes she has to watch.

Use the table at the right to solve Problems 21–23.

21. Estimate the total number of books the school received by rounding each number to the nearest hundred.

Jefferson Elementary School Books Received	
Math	436
Reading	352

22. Estimate the total number of books the school received by rounding each number to the nearest ten.

23. Find the total number of math and reading books. Which of your estimates is closer to the actual total?

► **Reasonable Answers**

**Use rounding to decide if the answer is reasonable.
Write *yes* or *no*. Then find the answer to see if you
were correct.**

24. $93 - 29 = 64$

25. $113 + 57 = 140$

26. $83 + 19 = 102$

27. $336 + 258 = 594$

28. $438 - 158 = 280$

29. $437 + 199 = 536$

30. $725 - 235 = 590$

31. $249 + 573 = 822$

32. $542 - 167 = 475$

© Houghton Mifflin Harcourt Publishing Company

► **What's the Error?**

Dear Math Students,

Today my teacher asked me to estimate the answer to this problem:

Ms. Smith's class brought in 384 soup labels. Mr. Alvarez's class brought in 524 soup labels. About how many labels did the two classes bring in?

$$
\begin{array}{rcl}
384 & \rightarrow & 300 \\
+524 & \rightarrow & +500 \\
\hline
 & & 800
\end{array}
$$

About 800 soup labels were brought in.

Is my answer correct? If not, please correct my work and tell me what I did wrong.

Your friend,
Puzzled Penguin

33. Write an answer to Puzzled Penguin.

_____

_____

► **Estimate the Number of Objects**

Jar D has 100 Beans. Estimate how many beans are in the other jars.

34. Jar A

_____

35. Jar B

_____

36. Jar C

_____

Name   Date

CA CC Content Standards 3.NBT.2
Mathematical Practices MP.1, MP.3, MP.4

► Solve and Discuss

Solve each problem. Label your answer. Use your Mathboard or a separate sheet of paper.

1. Elena made necklaces for her friends. She used 586 green beads and 349 red beads. How many beads did Elena use in all?

_____

2. Fabrice has a collection of 485 basketball cards and 217 baseball cards. How many sports cards does Fabrice have in all?

_____

► ⟨PATH to FLUENCY⟩ Introduce Addition Methods

Tonya and Mark collect seashells. Tonya has 249 shells, and Mark has 386 shells. How many shells do they have in all?

Here are three ways to find the answer:

Show All Totals Method	New Groups Below Method	New Groups Above Method
249 + 386 ——— 500 120 + 15 ——— 635	249 + 386 ——— 635	¹ ¹ 249 + 386 ——— 635

Proof Drawing:

6 hundreds   3 tens   5 ones

► PATH to FLUENCY **Practice Addition Methods**

Solve each problem. Make proof drawings to show that your answers are correct.

3. Ryan has two stamp albums. One album has 554 stamps, and the other has 428 stamps. How many stamps does Ryan have in all?

_____

4. One week Ashley read 269 pages. The next week she read 236 pages. What is the total number of pages she read in the two weeks?

_____

5. The video store has 445 comedy videos and 615 drama videos. How many comedy and drama videos does the store have altogether?

_____

6. Ali has 128 photos of her pets and 255 photos of her family. How many photos does Ali have altogether?

_____

Explore Multidigit Addition

Name _____ Date _____

CA CC Content Standards 3.NBT.2
Mathematical Practices MP.1, MP.3, MP.4, MP.6

► PATH to FLUENCY **Solve and Discuss**

Solve each problem using a numerical method and a proof drawing.

1. There are 359 cars and 245 trucks in the parking garage. How many vehicles are in the garage?

_____

2. The Creepy Crawler exhibit at the science museum has 693 spiders and 292 centipedes. How many spiders and centipedes are there in all?

_____

3. On Saturday, 590 people went to the art museum. On Sunday, 355 went to the museum. How many people went to the museum altogether?

_____

4. There were 120 people on the ferry yesterday. Today the ferry had 767 people. How many people in all were on the ferry during the past two days?

_____

▶ What's the Error?

Dear Math Students,

Today I found the answer to 168 + 78, but I don't know if I added correctly. Please look at my work. Is my answer right? If not, please correct my work and tell what I did wrong.

$$\begin{array}{r} 168 \\ +\ 78 \\ \hline 948 \end{array}$$

Your friend,
Puzzled Penguin

5. Write an answer to Puzzled Penguin.

_____

_____

▶ PATH to FLUENCY Line Up the Places to Add

Write each addition vertically. Line up the places correctly. Then add and make a proof drawing.

6. 179 + 38 = _____

7. 650 + 345 = _____

8. 407 + 577 = _____

Discuss Addition Methods

4-9

Class Activity

Name _____   Date _____

CA CC Content Standards **3.NBT.2**
Mathematical Practices **MP.1, MP.2, MP.4**

► (PATH to FLUENCY) **Decide When to Group**

Decide which new groups you will make.
Then add to see if you were correct.

1.　　123 　+ 247	2.　　358 　+ 434	3.　　732 　+ 189	4.　　416 　+ 396

Add.

5.　　647 　+ 178	6.　　132 　+ 763	7.　　554 　+ 257	8.　　168 　+ 692

9.　　384 　+ 586	10.　　631 　+ 189	11.　　464 　+ 446	12.　　313 　+ 649

13. 576 + 265　　14. 389 + 511　　15. 568 + 219　　16. 137 + 284

Write an equation and solve the problem.

17. The first animated film at the movie theatre
    lasted 129 minutes. The second film lasted
    104 minutes. How many minutes in all did
    the two movies last?

_____

© Houghton Mifflin Harcourt Publishing Company

▶ Solve and Discuss

Write an equation and solve the problem.

Show Your Work.

18. Jacob has 347 basketball cards in his collection. He has 256 baseball cards. How many cards does he have altogether?

_____

19. Jasmine's family drove for two days to visit her grandparents. They drove 418 miles on the first day and 486 miles on the second day. How many miles did they drive in all?

_____

20. The florist ordered 398 roses and 562 tulips. How many flowers did the florist order in all?

_____

21. Emilio checked a suitcase at the airport. His suitcase weighed 80 pounds. His wife checked three suitcases. Each of her suitcases weighed 30 pounds. How many pounds in all did their suitcases weigh?

_____

22. Write and solve an addition word problem where 287 and 614 are addends.

_____

_____

_____

The Grouping Concept in Addition

CA CC Content Standards **3.NBT.1, 3.NBT.2**
Mathematical Practices **MP.1, MP.4**

Name _____   **Date** _____

▶ Add Three-Digit Numbers

School Carnival Rides

Rides	Tickets Sold
Twister	298
Monster Mix	229
Crazy Coaster	193
Mega Wheel	295
Bumper Cars	301

Write an equation and solve the problem.

Show Your Work.

1. How many people went on the two most popular rides?

   _____

2. The total tickets sold for which two rides was 494?

   _____

3. Tickets for the Monster Mix and Crazy Coaster sold for $2. How much money did the school earn on the ticket sales for these two rides?

   _____

4. About how many tickets were sold for Twister, Monster Mix, and Mega Wheel altogether?

   _____

5. The total tickets sold for which three rides equals about 900?

   _____

► Use Addition to Solve Problems

Student Collections

Type of Collection	Number of Objects
rocks	403
stamps	371
shells	198
buttons	562
miniature cars	245

Write an equation and solve the problem.

Show Your Work.

6. How many objects are in the two smallest collections?

_____

7. The total number of objects in two collections is 760. What are the collections?

_____

8. Are the combined collections of shells and buttons greater than or less than the combined collections of rocks and stamps?

_____

9. Is the estimated sum of stamps, shells, and miniature cars closer to 700 or to 800?

_____

10. Suppose another student has a collection of sports cards. The number of sports cards is 154 greater than the number of rocks. How many cards are in the sports cards collection?

_____

Practice Addition

▶ **PATH to FLUENCY** **Discuss Subtraction Methods**

Solve this word problem.

> Mr. Kim had 134 jazz CDs. He sold 58 of them at his garage sale. How many jazz CDs does he have now?

1. Write a subtraction that you could do to answer this question.

_____

2. Make a place value drawing for 134. Take away 58. How many are left?

3. Write a numerical solution method for what you did in the drawing.

4. Describe how you ungrouped to subtract.

_____

_____

_____

_____

Name _____ Date _____

► **What's the Error?**

Dear Math Students,

Today I found the answer to 134 − 58, but I don't know if I did it correctly. Please look at my work. Is my answer right? If not, please correct my work and tell what I did wrong.

$$\begin{array}{r} 134 \\ -58 \\ \hline 124 \end{array}$$

Your friend,
Puzzled Penguin

5. Write an answer to Puzzled Penguin.

_____

_____

► **PATH to FLUENCY Subtraction Detective**

To avoid making subtraction mistakes, look at the top number closely. Do all the **ungrouping** you need to *before* you **subtract**. The magnifying glass around the top number helps you remember to be a "subtraction detective."

Subtract. Show your ungroupings numerically and with proof drawings.

6. 371 − 86

7. 163 − 47

8. 459 − 175

9. 277 − 68

Ungroup to Subtract

4-12
Class Activity

Name

Date

CA CC Content Standards **3.NBT.2**
Mathematical Practices **MP.1, MP.2, MP.4**

► PATH to FLUENCY **Ungroup to Subtract**

Solve each problem. Show your work numerically and with proof drawings.

1. Lakesha bought a box of 500 paper clips. So far, she has used 138 of them. How many are left?

_____

2. A movie theater has 400 seats. At the noon show, 329 seats were filled. How many seats were empty?

_____

3. At the start of the school year, Seiko had a brand new box of 300 crayons. Now 79 crayons are broken. How many unbroken crayons does Seiko have?

_____

► (PATH to FLUENCY) **Subtract Across Zeros**

Solve each problem. Show your work numerically and with proof drawings.

4. The students at Freedom Elementary School have a goal of reading 900 books. They have read 342 books. How many books do the students have left to read?

_____

5. There are 500 fiction books in the Lee School Library. There are 179 fewer non-fiction books than fiction books. How many books are non-fiction?

_____

6. The students at Olympia Elementary School collected 1,000 bottles for recycling. The students at Sterling Elementary collected 768 bottles. How many more bottles did the students at Olympia collect?

_____

▶ (PATH to FLUENCY) **Practice Subtracting Across Zeros**

Subtract. Make proof drawings for Exercises 7–10 on MathBoards or on a separate sheet of paper.

7. $\begin{array}{r} 800 \\ -391 \\ \hline \end{array}$

8. $\begin{array}{r} 500 \\ -333 \\ \hline \end{array}$

9. $\begin{array}{r} 400 \\ -217 \\ \hline \end{array}$

10. $\begin{array}{r} 900 \\ -818 \\ \hline \end{array}$

11. $\begin{array}{r} 600 \\ -575 \\ \hline \end{array}$

12. $\begin{array}{r} 700 \\ -248 \\ \hline \end{array}$

13. $\begin{array}{r} 200 \\ -109 \\ \hline \end{array}$

14. $\begin{array}{r} 800 \\ -519 \\ \hline \end{array}$

15. Math Journal Write a word problem that is solved by subtracting a 2-digit number from a 3-digit number that has a zero in both the ones and tens places. Then solve the problem.

▶ PATH to FLUENCY **Practice Deciding When to Ungroup**

Subtract. Make proof drawings if you need to on MathBoards or on a separate sheet of paper.

16. 912 − 265

17. 323 − 147

18. 280 − 136

19. 489 − 263

20. 754
    − 389

21. 912
    − 437

22. 341
    − 178

23. 603
    − 464

4-13

Class Activity

Name _____

Date _____

CA CC Content Standards 3.NBT.2
Mathematical Practices MP.1, MP.2

► (PATH to FLUENCY) **Ungroup from Left or Right**

Tony and Maria each solved this problem:

On Tuesday morning, a music store had 463 copies
of the new School Daze CD. By the end of the day,
they had sold 275 copies. How many copies were left?

Tony	**Maria**
Tony started ungrouping from the left.	Maria started ungrouping from the right.
1. He has enough hundreds.	**1.** She does not have enough ones. She ungroups 1 ten to make 10 more ones.
2. He does not have enough tens. He ungroups 1 hundred to make 10 more tens.	
	**2.** She does not have enough tens. She ungroups 1 hundred to get 10 more tens.
3. He does not have enough ones. He ungroups 1 ten to make 10 more ones.	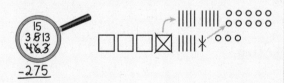
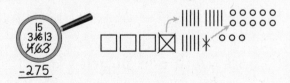	**3.** She has enough hundreds.
4. Complete the subtraction.	**4.** Complete the subtraction.
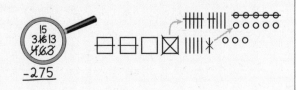	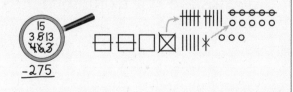

► PATH to FLUENCY **Choose a Method to Subtract**

Subtract.

1. 686
   − 387

2. 340
   − 167

3. 765
   − 498

4. 841
   − 253

5. 912
   − 575

6. 853
   − 194

7. 705
   − 429

8. 998
   − 299

9. 513
   − 156

10. 627 − 348

11. 544 − 169

12. 810 − 261

Solve.

13. Rochelle is putting 302 digital photos in an album. Of these, 194 are from her trip to the Grand Canyon. How many photos are not from Rochelle's trip?

14. There were 645 bicycles in a race. Toby finished eighty-seventh. How many bicycles finished after Toby?

Name _____   **Date** _____

CA CC Content Standards 3.NBT.2
Mathematical Practices MP.1, MP.2, MP.4

▶ (PATH to FLUENCY) **Relate Addition and Subtraction**

**Solve each problem. Make a proof drawing
if you need to.**

1. There were 138 students in the gym for the
   assembly. Then 86 more students came in. How
   many students were in the gym altogether?

   _____

2. There were 224 students in the gym for the
   assembly. Then 86 students left. How many
   students were still in the gym?

   _____

3. Look at your addition, subtraction, and proof
   drawings from Problems 1 and 2. How are
   addition and subtraction related?

   _____

   _____

   _____

▶ **Solve and Discuss**

Solve. Label your answers.

Show your work.

4. Marly had 275 baseball cards. Her brother gave her a collection of 448 baseball cards. How many baseball cards does Marly have now?

_____

5. Write a subtraction word problem related to the addition word problem in Problem 4. Then find the answer without doing any calculations.

_____

_____

_____

_____

6. Bill drove 375 miles on the first day of his cross-country trip. The next day he drove an additional 528 miles. How many miles did Bill drive on the first two days of his trip?

_____

7. Write a subtraction problem related to the addition word problem in Problem 6. Then find the answer without doing any calculations.

_____

_____

_____

4-15
Class Activity

Name

Date

CA CC Content Standards **3.NBT.2**
Mathematical Practices **MP.1, MP.2**

▶ Subtract and Check

Solve each problem.

Show Your Work.

1. Ken collects photographs as a hobby. He has 375 photographs in his collection at home. If Ken brought 225 of his photographs to share with his classmates, how many photographs did he leave at home?

2. Of the 212 third- and fourth-grade students, 165 attended the school festival. How many students did not attend the festival?

3. Becky's mom has 653 CDs in her collection. Becky's aunt has 438 CDs in her collection. How many more CDs does Becky's mom have than Becky's aunt?

4. Andrea and John need 750 tickets to get a board game. They have 559 tickets. How many more tickets do they need?

► PATH to FLUENCY **Practice Deciding When to Ungroup**

Answer each question.

Adair subtracted 595 from 834.

5. Did she have to ungroup to make more tens? Explain.

_____

_____

_____

6. Did she have to ungroup to make more ones? Explain.

_____

_____

_____

Beatrice subtracted 441 from 950.

7. Did she have to ungroup to make more tens? Explain.

_____

_____

_____

8. Did she have to ungroup to make more ones? Explain.

_____

_____

_____

Wan subtracted 236 from 546.

9. Did he have to ungroup to make more tens? Explain.

_____

_____

_____

10. Did he have to ungroup to make more ones? Explain.

_____

_____

_____

Name _____ Date _____

CA CC Content Standards 3.NBT.2
Mathematical Practices MP.1, MP.2

►  PATH to FLUENCY **Practice Addition and Subtraction**

Add or subtract.

1. 112
    + 459

2. 572
    − 357

3. 253
    + 328

4. 710
    − 464

5. 461
    − 182

6. 540
    + 175

7. 921
    − 653

8. 398
    − 99

9. 712
    + 189

10. 600
     − 223

11. 809
     − 576

12. 634
     + 287

Solve.

13. The height of Angeline Falls in Washington is 450 feet. Snoqualmie Falls in Washington is 182 feet lower than Angeline Falls. What is the height of Snoqualmie Falls?

14. Jill scored 534 points at the arcade on Friday night. She scored 396 points on Saturday night. How many points did she score altogether?

▶ **Solve Real World Problems**

The students at Liberty Elementary collected pennies for a fundraiser.

Pennies Collected	
Grade	**Number of Pennies**
Grade 1	225
Grade 2	436
Grade 3	517
Grade 4	609
Grade 5	342

Write an equation and solve the problem.

Show Your Work.

15. How many pennies did Grades 2 and 5 collect?

_____

16. How many more pennies did Grades 1 and 3 collect than Grade 4?

_____

17. Is the total number of pennies collected by Grades 1 and 4 greater than or less than the total number collected by Grades 3 and 5?

_____

18. The total number of pennies collected by which three grades equals about 1,000?

_____

19. Suppose the kindergarten students collected 198 fewer pennies than the Grade 3 students. How many pennies would the kindergarteners have collected?

_____

Addition and Subtraction Practice

CA CC Content Standards **3.OA.8, 3.NBT.1, 3.NBT.2**
Mathematical Practices **MP.1, MP.2**

Name _____ **Date** _____

▶ Solve Multistep Word Problems

Solve each problem. Label your answers.

Show your work.

1. Isabel bought 36 pieces of fruit for her soccer team. There are 16 apples, 12 bananas, and the rest are pears. How many pieces of fruit are pears?

    _____

2. Toby has a collection of sports cards. He had 13 baseball cards, 16 basketball cards, and 14 football cards. Toby sold 15 cards and he bought 17 hockey cards. What is the total number of cards in Toby's collection now?

    _____

3. There are 15 more boys than girls in the school band. There are 27 girls. How many students are in the school band?

    _____

4. Finn delivered 13 pizzas. Then he delivered 8 more pizzas. Altogether, he delivered 6 fewer pizzas than Liz. How many pizzas did Liz deliver?

    _____

5. Majeed built 7 car models and 14 airplane models. Jasmine built 9 more car models than Majeed and 6 fewer airplane models. How many models did Jasmine build in all?

    _____

► Reasonable Answers

**Use rounding to decide if the answer is reasonable. Write
yes or *no*. Then find the answer to see if you were correct.**

6. Nathan counted 28 large dogs and 37 small dogs
   at the dog park. He said he saw 55 dogs in all.

   _____

7. There are 122 third-and fourth-grade students at
   Cedar Creek Elementary School. There are 67 students
   in third grade and 55 students in fourth grade.

   _____

8. The pet supermarket sold 245 bags of dog food and
   167 bags of cat food. The supermarket sold 312 bags
   of pet food in all.

   _____

9. The total distance from Charleston, West Virginia
   to Biloxi, Mississippi is 913 miles. Benjamin drove
   455 miles from Charleston to Athens, Georgia.
   Then he drove 458 miles from Athens to Biloxi.

   _____

10. There were 432 people at the basketball game.
    257 people sat on the home team side. 175 people
    sat on the visiting team side.

    _____

11. The Pecos River is 234 miles longer than the
    Yellowstone River. The Yellowstone River is
    692 miles long. The Pecos River is 826 miles long.

    _____

Solve Word Problems

Name _____   Date _____

CA CC Content Standards **3.NBT.1, 3.NBT.2**
Mathematical Practices **MP.1, MP.2, MP.4, MP.5**

▶ Math and Maps

The Pony Express was a mail service from St. Joseph,
Missouri, to Sacramento, California. The Pony Express
service carried mail by horseback riders in relays.

**Use the information on the map for Problems 1–3.
Write an equation and solve the problem.**

1. How many miles did the Pony Express riders travel
   on a trip from Sacramento to Salt Lake City?

   _____

2. The total distance from St. Joseph to Fort Laramie
   is 616 miles. How many miles is it from Julesburg
   to Fort Laramie?

   _____

3. Write and solve a problem that can be answered
   using the map.

   _____

   _____

► Use a Table

It took the Pony Express 10 days to deliver letters between Sacramento and St. Joseph. Today we send emails that are delivered within a few minutes. The chart below shows the number of emails sent in a month by different students.

Number of Emails Sent last Month					
Name	Robbie	Samantha	Ellen	Bryce	Callie
Number	528	462	942	388	489

Use the information in the table for Problems 4–6. Write an equation and solve the problem.

4. How many more emails did Robbie send than Callie?

_____

5. How many more emails did Ellen send than Bryce and Samantha combined?

_____

6. Tamara said that Robbie and Bryce together sent 806 emails. Is her answer reasonable? Explain. Then find the actual answer to see if you are correct.

_____

_____

Focus on Mathematical Practices

Name _____ **Date** _____

1. Select the way that shows three hundred fifty-seven. Mark all that apply.

   Ⓐ 357

   Ⓑ 3 hundreds + 57 tens

   Ⓒ 3 hundreds + 5 tens + 7 ones

   Ⓓ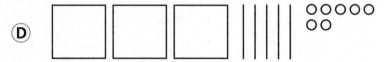

   Ⓔ 300 + 5 + 7

2. Make a place value drawing for the number.

   691

   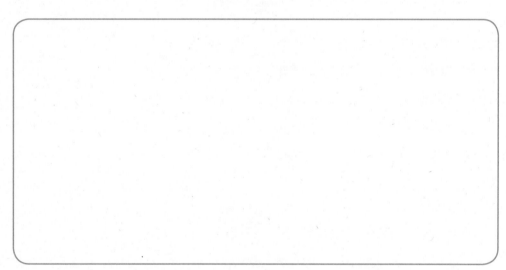

3. A shop sells 564 posters. It sells 836 calendars. Round each number to the nearest ten to estimate about how many more calendars the shop sells than posters.

   about _____ more calendars

4. Write the number in the box that shows how it should be rounded to the nearest hundred.

| 479 | 440 | 655 | 405 | 643 |

400	500	600	700

5. For numbers 5a–5e, use rounding to decide whether the answer is reasonable. Choose Yes or No.

5a. $187 - 43 = 144$ ○ Yes   ○ No

5b. $328 + 87 = 385$ ○ Yes   ○ No

5c. $652 + 189 = 841$ ○ Yes   ○ No

5d. $1,293 - 126 = 367$ ○ Yes   ○ No

5e. $2,946 - 488 = 2,458$ ○ Yes   ○ No

6. Choose the difference that completes the number sentence.

$$425 - 346 = \begin{array}{|c|} \hline 79 \\ 89 \\ 121 \\ 771 \\ \hline \end{array}$$

7. Subtract.

$700 - 255 =$

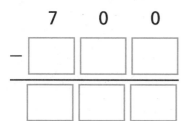

8. Add.

$\begin{array}{r} 521 \\ + 129 \\ \hline \end{array}$

(A) 640   (C) 650

(B) 641   (D) 651

For numbers 9 and 10, add or subtract. Make a proof drawing to show that your answer is correct.

9. $\begin{array}{r} 497 \\ + 326 \\ \hline \end{array}$

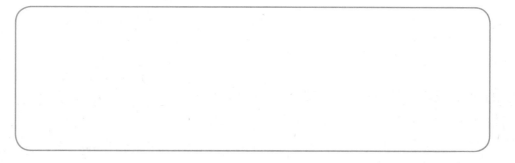

10. $\begin{array}{r} 690 \\ - 493 \\ \hline \end{array}$

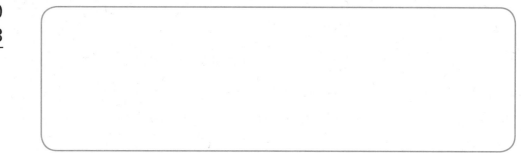

For numbers 11 and 12, add or subtract. *Show your work.*

11.   437
    + 273

Which method did you use to add?

New Groups Above
New Groups Below
Show All Totals

I used the ⎡ ... ⎤ method.

12.   617
    − 549

Did you ungroup to subtract? Explain why or why not.

13. Andre buys 860 bricks. He buys 575 red bricks and 147 tan bricks. The rest of the bricks are gray. Write and solve an equation to find how many gray bricks Andre buys.

Equation: _____

_____ gray bricks

What if Andre returns 248 red bricks, 85 tan bricks, and 58 gray bricks? How many bricks does Andre have now?

_____ bricks

14. Pia collects 245 acorns in a jar. For numbers 14a–14d, select True or False for each statement.

   14a. Pia collects 193 more acorns.
   She now has 338 acorns.   ○ True   ○ False

   14b. Pia gives 160 acorns to Ana.
   She now has 85 acorns.   ○ True   ○ False

   14c. Pia collects 286 more acorns.
   She uses 143 to decorate a tray.
   She now has 388 acorns.   ○ True   ○ False

   14d. Pia gives her two sisters 85 acorns
   each. She now has 160 acorns.   ○ True   ○ False

15. Li earns 321 points in the first round of a math
   contest. He earns another 278 points in the second
   round and 315 points in the third round. Li says he
   has 804 points.

   Is Li's answer reasonable? Explain.

   Find the actual answer to check if you are correct.

16. Darian sells 293 bags of popcorn and 321 bags of peanuts.

Part A

How many bags of popcorn and peanuts does Darian sell?

_____ bags

Part B

Write a subtraction word problem related to how many bags of popcorn and peanuts Darian sells. Then find the answer without doing any calculations.

17. A zoo has 209 reptiles. There are 93 lizards and 52 turtles. The rest are snakes. How many snakes are at the zoo?

_____ snakes

Family Letter

Content Overview

Dear Family,

In this unit, your child will solve addition, subtraction, multiplication, and division problems involving unknown addends and factors.

- If one of the addends is unknown, it can be found by subtracting the known addend from the total or by counting on from the known addend to the total.
- If the total is unknown, it can be found by adding the addends.
- If one of the factors is unknown, it can be found by dividing the product by the other factor.
- If the product is unknown, it can be found by multiplying the factors.

Math Mountains are used to show a total and two addends. Students can use the Math Mountain to write an equation and then solve the equation to find the unknown.

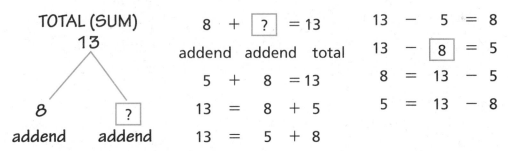

TOTAL (SUM)
13

8   ?
addend   addend

$$8 + \boxed{?} = 13$$
addend addend total

$$5 + 8 = 13$$

$$13 = 8 + 5$$

$$13 = 5 + 8$$

$$13 - 5 = 8$$

$$13 - \boxed{8} = 5$$

$$8 = 13 - 5$$

$$5 = 13 - 8$$

Equations with numbers alone on the left are also emphasized to help with the understanding of algebra.

Comparison Bars are used to solve problems that involve one amount that is more than or less than another amount. Drawing Comparison Bars can help a student organize the information in the problem in order to find the unknown smaller amount, the unknown larger amount, or the difference.

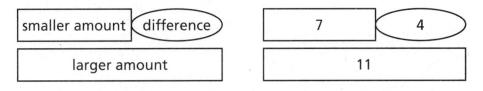

smaller amount	difference
larger amount	

7	4
11	

Please call or write if you have any questions or comments.

Sincerely,
Your child's teacher

CA CC

Unit 5 addresses the following standards from the *Common Core State Standards for Mathematics with California Additions*: **3.0A.3, 3.0A.4, 3.0A.8, 3.NBT.1, 3.NBT.2** and for all Mathematical Practices.

Estimada familia:

En esta unidad, su niño resolverá sumas, restas, multiplicaciones y divisiones con sumandos o factores desconocidos.

- Si uno de los sumandos se desconoce, puede hallarse restando el sumando conocido del total, o contando hacia adelante desde el sumando conocido hasta llegar al total.

- Si el total se desconoce, puede hallarse sumando los sumandos.

- Si uno de los factores se desconoce, puede hallarse dividiendo el producto entre el otro factor.

- Si el producto se desconoce, puede hallarse multiplicando los factores.

Para mostrar un total y dos sumandos se usan las **Montañas matemáticas**. Los estudiantes puede usarlas para escribir una ecuación, y al resolverla, hallar el elemento desconocido.

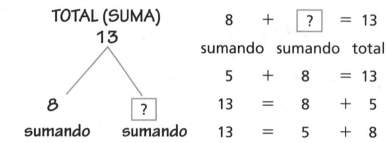

$$8 + \boxed{?} = 13$$

sumando sumando total

$$5 + 8 = 13$$

$$13 = 8 + 5$$

$$13 = 5 + 8$$

$$13 - 5 = 8$$

$$13 - \boxed{8} = 5$$

$$8 = 13 - 5$$

$$5 = 13 - 8$$

Se hace énfasis en las ecuaciones que tienen números solos en el lado izquierdo, para facilitar la comprensión del álgebra.

Para resolver problemas con una cantidad que es más o menos que otra, se usan **Barras de comparación**. Estas barras sirven para organizar la información del problema, y hallar así, la cantidad desconocida más pequeña, la más grande o la diferencia.

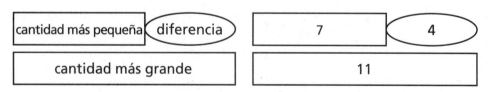

Si tiene alguna pregunta o algún comentario, por favor comuníquese conmigo.

Atentamente,
El maestro de su niño

 CA CC

En la Unidad 5 se aplican los siguientes estándares auxiliares, contenidos en los *Estándares estatales comunes de matemáticas con adiciones para California*: **3.OA.3, 3.OA.4, 3.OA.8, 3.NBT.1, 3.NBT.2** y todos los de prácticas matemáticas.

© Houghton Mifflin Harcourt Publishing Company

Addition and Subtraction Situations

Name _____ Date _____

CA CC Content Standards **3.NBT.2**
Mathematical Practices **MP.1, MP.2, MP.4, MP.5, MP.7**

VOCABULARY
total
addend
sum

▶ Math Mountains and Equations

Complete.

1. Look at the Math Mountain and the 8 equations.
What relationships do you see? In each equation,
label each number as an **addend** (*A*) or the **total** (*T*).

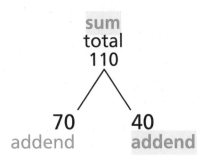

sum
total
110

70   40
addend   addend

$110 = 70 + 40$ $70 + 40 = 110$

___ ___ ___   ___ ___ ___

$110 = 40 + 70$ $40 + 70 = 110$

___ ___ ___   ___ ___ ___

$40 = 110 - 70$ $110 - 70 = 40$

___ ___ ___   ___ ___ ___

$70 = 110 - 40$ $110 - 40 = 70$

___ ___ ___   ___ ___ ___

2. Write the 8 equations for this Math Mountain.
Label each number as the total (*T*) or an addend (*A*).

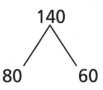

140

80   60

_____   _____

_____   _____

_____   _____

_____   _____

Name _____   Date _____

▶ Solve and Discuss

Solve each problem. Label your answers.

3. **Add To** Chris's group picked 80 apples. His mother's group picked 60 more. How many apples do they have now?

   _____

4. **Take From** Chris's group had 140 apples. They ate 80 of them. How many apples do they have now?

   _____

5. **Put Together/Take Apart** Alison's class brought 70 juice boxes to the picnic. Taylor's class brought 50 juice boxes. How many juice boxes did they bring altogether?

   _____

6. **Put Together/Take Apart** There are 120 juice boxes at the picnic. Alison puts 70 on tables and leaves the rest in the cooler. How many juice boxes are in the cooler?

   _____

Addition and Subtraction Situations

► Represent Word Problems with Math Tools

The equations and Math Mountains below
show the word problems on page 274.

Add To

80   +   60   =   ☐

Chris's   Mom's   total
group   group

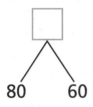

80   60

Take From

140   −   80   =   ☐

total   ate   now
(sum)

140

80   ☐

Put Together/Take Apart

70   +   50   =   ☐

Alison's   Taylor's   total
class   class

70   50

Put Together/Take Apart

120   −   70   =   ☐

total   tables   cooler

70   +   ☐   =   120

tables   cooler   total

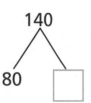

120

70   ☐

7. Write the unknown numbers in the boxes.

8. How are these math tools the same?
   How are they different?

_____

9. **Math Journal** Write a word problem for this
   equation: 110 − 40 = ☐. Then solve it.

VOCABULARY
expression
equation

▶ (PATH to FLUENCY) **Discuss the = and ≠ Signs**

An **expression** is a combination of numbers, variables, and/or operation signs. Expressions do not have an equal sign.

An **equation** is made up of two equal quantities or expressions. An equal sign (=) is used to show that the two sides are equal.

$$8 = 5 + 3 \qquad 4 + 2 = 6 \qquad 7 = 7 \qquad 3 + 2 = 2 + 3 \qquad 6 - 2 = 1 + 1 + 2$$

The "is not equal to" sign (≠) shows that two quantities are not equal.

$$7 \neq 5 + 3 \qquad 4 + 2 \neq 8 \qquad 7 \neq 6 \qquad 6 - 2 \neq 2 + 3 \qquad 5 + 2 \neq 1 + 1 + 3$$

10. Use the = sign to write four equations. Vary how many numbers you have on each side of the sign.

_____

_____

_____

_____

11. Use the ≠ sign to write four "is not equal to" statements. Vary how many numbers you have on each side of the sign.

_____

_____

_____

_____

Write a number to make the number sentence true.

12. $160 = \boxed{} + 90$

13. $30 + \boxed{} \neq 120$

14. $70 + 20 = 20 + \boxed{}$

15. $150 - \boxed{} = 70$

16. $\boxed{} \neq 140 - 70$

17. $60 - 20 \neq 10 + 10 + \boxed{}$

Write = or ≠ to make a true number sentence.

18. $80 + 20 + 40 \underline{} 90 + 50$

19. $80 \underline{} 60 - 20$

20. $70 \underline{} 40 + 30$

© Houghton Mifflin Harcourt Publishing Company

Addition and Subtraction Situations

CA CC Content Standards 3.NBT.2, 3.OA.3, 3.OA.4
Mathematical Practices MP.1, MP.2, MP.4, MP.5

▶ Solve Unknown Addend Word Problems

Draw a Math Mountain and write and label an equation with a variable. Then solve each problem.

Show your work.

1. **Put Together/Take Apart:**
   Unknown Addend Stacy invited 90 girls and some boys to her party. 160 children were invited in all. How many boys were invited?

   _____

2. **Put Together/Take Apart:**
   Unknown Addend There were 150 people at the park. 70 were playing soccer. The others were playing softball. How many people were playing softball?

   _____

3. **Add To: Unknown Addend** Jan planted 80 tulips last week. Today she planted some lilies. Now she has 170 flowers. How many lilies did she plant?

   _____

4. **Take From: Unknown Addend** Tim's team had 140 tennis balls. Then his brother's team borrowed some. Now Tim's team has 60 tennis balls. How many did his brother's team borrow?

   _____

▶ Represent Unknown Addends with Math Tools

The equations and Math Mountains below show
the word problems on page 277.

**Put Together/Take Apart:
Unknown Addend**

$$90 + b = 160$$
girls · boys · children

children
160

90 | [ ]
girls · boys

**Put Together/Take Apart:
Unknown Addend**

$$150 - s = 70$$
park · softball · soccer

park
150

[ ] | 70
softball · soccer

Add To: Unknown Addend

$$80 + l = 170$$
tulips · lilies · flowers

flowers
170

80 | [ ]
tulips · lilies

Take From: Unknown Addend

$$140 - n = 60$$
balls · some · now

balls
140

[ ] | 60
some · now

5. Write the unknown numbers in the boxes and above the variables.

6. How are these math tools alike? How are they different?

► Solve Unknown Factor Word Problems

Write an equation for each word problem.
Use a variable to represent the unknown
factor. Then solve the problem.

Show Your Work.

7. A toymaker has 36 boxes of toy trains to
   ship to 4 toy shops. Each shop will get the
   same number of boxes. How many boxes
   of toy trains will each shop get?

   _____

8. There are 56 cars in a parking lot. There are
   8 rows and the same number of cars is in
   each row. How many cars are in each row?

   _____

9. An apartment building has 42 apartments.
   There are 6 apartments on each floor.
   How many floors are in the apartment building?

   _____

10. There are 48 students in the marching band.
    The students stand in equal rows of 8.
    How many rows of students are there?

    _____

▶ Solve Unknown Factor Word Problems (continued)

**Write an equation for each word problem.
Use a variable to represent the unknown
factor. Then solve the problem.**

Show Your Work.

11. Daniel is setting up seats for the third
grade play. There are 6 seats in each row.
There are 54 seats in all. How many rows
of seats are there?

_____

12. Mrs. Martinez is sewing buttons on
4 costumes. Each costume has the same
number of buttons. There are 32 buttons
in all. How many buttons are on each costume?

_____

13. The library received 63 new books.
The librarian will put 7 books on each
shelf. How many shelves are there?

_____

14. There are 72 juice boxes for the class
picnic. The juice boxes are in packs of 8.
How many packs of juice boxes are there?

_____

Word Problems with Unknown Addends or Unknown Factors

Name _____ Date _____

CA CC Content Standards **3.NBT.2, 3.OA.3, 3.OA.4**
Mathematical Practices **MP.1, MP.2, MP.4, MP.5**

▶ Solve Unknown Start Problems

Solve each problem. Label your answers.   *Show your work.*

1. **Add To: Unknown Start** Greta puts some beads on a string. Then she puts on 70 more beads. Now there are 130 beads on the string. How many beads did she put on the string to start?

    _____

2. **Take From: Unknown Start** Greta puts some beads on a string. Seventy of the beads fell off the string. Sixty beads are still on the string. How many beads were there at first?

    _____

3. **Add To: Unknown Start** Patrick was carrying some booklets. His teacher asked him to carry 30 more booklets. Now he has 110 booklets. How many booklets did he start with?

    _____

4. **Take From: Unknown Start** Patricia was carrying some pencils. Her friend took 30 of them. Patricia has 80 pencils left. How many pencils was she carrying at first?

    _____

VOCABULARY
situation equation
solution equation

► Represent Unknown Start Problems with Math Tools

The equations and Math Mountains below show the word problems on page 281.

Add To: Unknown Start

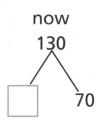

now
130

start   more

situation equation:

$\square + 70 = 130$

start   more   now

solution equation:

$70 + \square = 130$

$130 - 70 = \square$

Take From: Unknown Start

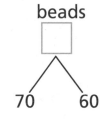

beads

70   60

fell   on
off

situation equation:

$\square - 70 = 60$

beads   fell   on
          off

solution equation:

$60 + 70 = \square$

Add To: Unknown Start

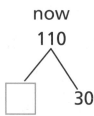

now
110

start   more

situation equation:

$\square + 30 = 110$

start   more   now

solution equations:

$30 + \square = 110$

$110 - 30 = \square$

Take From: Unknown Start

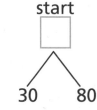

start

30   80

friend   now

situation equation:

$\square - 30 = 80$

start   friend   now

solution equation:

$80 + 30 = \square$

5. Write the unknown numbers in the boxes.

6. How are these math tools alike? How are they different?

_____

_____

▶ Write Situation and Solution Equations

**Write a situation equation and a solution equation.
Then solve the problem.**

7. Eight vans with the same number of students
in each van took 40 students to the science center
for a field trip. How many students were in each van?

   Situation Equation: _____

   Solution Equation: _____

8. Fiona made some barrettes. She put 9 beads
on each barrette. If she used 63 beads, how many
barrettes did she make?

   Situation Equation: _____

   Solution Equation: _____

9. The pet store has 81 birds. There are 9 birds in
each cage. How many cages are there?

   Situation Equation: _____

   Solution Equation: _____

10. Enrique has 56 miniature cars. He put the
same number of cars on 7 shelves in his
room. How many cars are on each shelf?

   Situation Equation: _____

   Solution Equation: _____

▶ Write Situation and Solution Equations (continued)

**Write a situation equation and a solution equation.
Then solve the problem.**

11. A group of 48 students from 8 schools are competing in the science fair. Each school sends the same number of students. How many students are competing from each school?

    Situation Equation: _____

    Solution Equation: _____

12. An array on one wall in an art gallery has 27 photographs. Each row has 9 photographs. How many rows are there?

    Situation Equation: _____

    Solution Equation: _____

13. Jody bought 4 bags of lemons to make lemonade. The same number of lemons was in each bag. There were a total of 36 lemons. How many lemons were in each bag?

    Situation Equation: _____

    Solution Equation: _____

14. A hardware store sold a number of furnace filters. There were 6 filters in each box. If they sold 54 furnace filters, how many boxes of filters did the hardware store sell?

    Situation Equation: _____

    Solution Equation: _____

Word Problems with Unknown Starts

Name _____ Date _____

CA CC Content Standards **3.NBT.1, 3.NBT.2**
Mathematical Practices **MP.1, MP.2, MP.4, MP.8**

▶ Compare Numbers

Compare the numbers. Write >, < or = in each ◯.

1. 34 ◯ 86

2. 97 ◯ 67

3. 653 ◯ 663

4. 875 ◯ 587

5. 752 ◯ 572

6. 864 ◯ 846

7. 1,932 ◯ 2,951

8. 2,633 ◯ 2,487

9. 3,478 ◯ 3,478

10. 4,786 ◯ 4,876

▶ Order Numbers

Write the numbers in order from greatest to least.

11. 69, 20, 81

12. 381, 124, 197

_____

_____

Write the numbers in order from least to greatest.

13. 2,245, 1,642, 787

14. 1,987, 1,898, 1,789

_____

_____

▶ Discuss Comparison Problems

Solve each problem. Label your answers.

David has 5 marbles. Ana has 8 marbles.

15. How many more marbles
    does Ana have than David? _____

16. How many fewer marbles
    does David have than Ana? _____

Here are two ways to represent the comparison situation.

Comparison Drawing

David ○ ○ ○ ○ ○
      │ │ │ │ │
Ana ○ ○ ○ ○ ○ ○ ○ ○

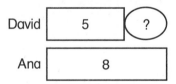

Comparison Bars

| David | 5 | ? |
| Ana | 8 | |

Claire has 8 marbles. Sasha has 15 marbles.

Show your work.

17. How many more marbles does
    Sasha have than Claire? _____

18. How many fewer marbles does
    Claire have than Sasha? _____

Rocky has 7 fishing lures. Megan has 12 fishing lures.

19. How many fewer fishing
    lures does Rocky have
    than Megan? _____

Comparison Problems

► Comparison Problems With an Unknown Larger or Smaller Amount

Solve each problem. Label your answers.

Show your work.

20. **Unknown Larger Amount** Maribel has 18 stickers. Arnon has 13 more stickers than Maribel. How many stickers does Arnon have?

_____

21. **Unknown Smaller Amount** Arnon has 31 stickers. Maribel has 13 fewer stickers than Arnon. How many stickers does Maribel have?

_____

22. **Unknown Larger Amount** Ivan has 19 goldfish. Milo has 15 more goldfish than Ivan. How many goldfish does Milo have?

_____

23. **Unknown Smaller Amount** Milo has 34 goldfish. Ivan has 15 fewer goldfish than Milo. How many goldfish does Ivan have?

_____

► Use Comparison Bars to Represent an Unknown Amount

Solve each problem. Label your answers.

Show your work.

24. **Unknown Smaller Amount** T.J. has 18 fewer miniature cars than Corey. Corey has 32 miniature cars. How many miniature cars does T.J. have?

_____

25. **Unknown Larger Amount** Corey has 18 more miniature cars than T.J. T.J. has 14 miniature cars. How many miniature cars does Corey have?

_____

26. **Unknown Smaller Amount** Grace has 19 fewer stuffed animals than Sophia. Sophia has 31 stuffed animals. How many stuffed animals does Grace have?

_____

27. **Unknown Larger Amount** Sophia has 19 more stuffed animals than Grace. Grace has 12 stuffed animals. How many stuffed animals does Sophia have?

_____

Comparison Problems

Name _____   Date _____

CA CC Content Standards **3.NBT.2**
Mathematical Practices **MP.1, MP.3, MP.6**

▶ What's the Error?

Dear Math Students,

As part of my math homework, I solved this problem:

Carlos has 19 fish. He has 14 fewer fish than Daniel. How many fish does Daniel have?

Here is what I did: 19 – 14 = 5

Is my answer right? If not, please correct my work, and tell me what I did wrong.

Your friend,
Puzzled Penguin

Daniel has 5 fish.

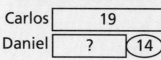

1. Write an answer to Puzzled Penguin.

_____

_____

▶ Solve Comparison Problems with Misleading Language

Solve each problem on a separate piece of paper.

2. Unknown Smaller Amount Daniel has 23 fish. He has 15 more fish than Carlos. How many fish does Carlos have?

3. Unknown Larger Amount Gina ran 12 laps. She ran 8 fewer laps than Bettina. How many laps did Bettina run?

4. Unknown Smaller Amount Bettina ran 20 laps. She ran 8 more laps than Gina. How many laps did Gina run?

5. Unknown Larger Amount Sara read 18 books this month. She read 13 fewer books than Lupe. How many books did Lupe read this month?

▶ Solve Comparison Problems Without the Words *More* or *Fewer*

Solve each problem. Label your answers.

Show your work.

6. The coach brought 18 hockey sticks to practice. There were 23 players at practice. How many players didn't get sticks?

_____

7. At a meeting, 15 people had to stand because there were not enough chairs. There were 12 chairs. How many people came to the meeting?

_____

8. Jess had 16 apples. After he gave one to each of his cousins, he had 13 apples left. How many cousins does Jess have?

_____

9. At the park, 4 of the children could not swing because there were not enough swings. There were 20 children at the park. How many swings were on the swing set?

_____

10. Maile took one step on each tile along the garden path. After she took 14 steps, there were 13 more tiles left to go. How many tiles were there along the path?

_____

▶ Solve Problems with Extra Information

Read each problem. Cross out any extra information. Then solve.

1. Emma solved 9 math problems and answered 7 reading questions. Her sister solved 8 math problems. How many math problems did they solve in all?

   _____

2. Mark had 6 shirts and 5 pairs of pants. Today his aunt gave him 4 more shirts and another pair of pants. How many shirts does he have now?

   _____

3. A parking lot had 179 cars and 95 trucks. Then 85 cars left the lot. How many cars are in the parking lot now?

   _____

4. Laura had some roses in a vase. From her garden, she picked 7 more roses and 6 daisies. Now she has 12 roses in all. How many roses did she have at first?

   _____

5. Nikko had 245 pennies and 123 nickels. His brother gave him 89 more pennies and 25 more nickels. How many pennies does Nikko have now?

   _____

► Solve Problems with Hidden Information

**Read each problem. Circle the hidden information.
Then solve.**

6. Samuel had 16 horseshoes in the shed
   yesterday. Today he put a new set of
   horseshoes on his horse Betsy. How many
   horseshoes are left in the shed?

   _____

7. Maya is going on a vacation with her family for
   a week and 3 days. How many days will she be
   on vacation?

   _____

8. Julie bought a dozen eggs at the market. She
   gave 3 of them to Serge. How many eggs does
   Julie have left?

   _____

9. Lisa had 3 quarters and 2 dimes. Then she
   found 3 nickels and 12 pennies. What is the
   value of the coins in cents she has now?

   _____

10. Marissa is moving away. She is going to move
    back in a year and 21 days. How many days will
    she be gone?

    _____

▶ Recognize Word Problems with Not Enough Information

Tell what information is needed to solve each problem.

11. Sara bought 8 bananas at the fruit market. She put them in a bowl with some oranges. How many pieces of fruit are in the bowl?

_____

_____

12. Rebecca did 112 dives in competition last summer. This summer, she did many more dives in competition. How many competition dives did she do in the two summers?

_____

_____

13. Meg bought 3 mystery books and put them on the shelf with her other mystery books. How many mystery books are now on the shelf?

_____

_____

14. Our school has 5 soccer balls, 6 basketballs, and 4 footballs. Today, some of the footballs were lost. How many balls does the school have now?

_____

_____

► Solve Word Problems with Not Enough Information

If more information is needed, rewrite the problem to include the necessary information. Then solve it.

15. Leah began fishing at 2:00 in the afternoon. She stopped at dinnertime. How many hours did Leah fish?

_____

_____

16. The train traveled 376 miles on Tuesday. It traveled even more miles on Wednesday. How many miles did the train travel on Tuesday and Wednesday?

_____

_____

17. The Kitchen Store sold 532 pans and 294 pots. Then some pans were returned. How many pans were not returned?

_____

_____

18. Julio and Scott played 6 card games and 4 computer games today. How many hours did they play games?

_____

_____

▶ Write First Step Questions

**Write the first step question and answer.
Then solve the problem.**

Show your work.

1. The orchard has 8 rows of apple trees. There are
   7 rows with 6 apple trees and one row with 4 apple
   trees. How many apple trees are in the orchard?

   _____

   _____

2. Ms. Hayes bought 4 packs of pencils with 10 pencils in
   each pack. She divided the pencils evenly among her
   5 children. How many pencils did each child get?

   _____

   _____

3. Kylen made 30 necklaces and gave 6 away. She put
   the rest in 4 boxes with an equal number in each
   box. How many necklaces were in each box?

   _____

   _____

4. Libby had 42 vacation pictures and 12 birthday pictures.
   She put an equal number of pictures on 9 pages in her
   scrapbook. How many pictures did Libby put on each page?

   _____

   _____

5. Mr. Cerda bought 9 boxes of tiles. Each box had 8 tiles.
   He used all but 5 of the tiles. How many tiles did
   Mr. Cerda use?

   _____

   _____

► Write First Step Questions (continued)

Write the first step question and answer. Then solve the problem.

Show your work.

6. A bus has 10 seats that can each hold 2 passengers and another seat that can hold 3 passengers. How many passengers can be seated on the bus?

_____

_____

7. Dana made 6 fruit baskets. She put 4 apples, 2 pears, and 3 oranges in each basket. How many pieces of fruit did Dana use in all?

_____

_____

8. Cecilia ordered 5 pizzas for a group of friends. Each pizza had 8 slices. All but 3 slices were eaten. How many slices were eaten?

_____

_____

9. Randall has 122 coins in his collection. Fifty coins are quarters and the rest are nickels. If he fills 9 pages in a coin folder with the same number of nickels, how many nickels are on each page?

_____

_____

10. Lindsey made 6 bracelets. She used a total of 60 beads. Each bracelet has 6 beads that are silver and the rest are blue. How many beads on each bracelet are blue?

_____

_____

Write First Step Questions for Two Step Problems

▶ What's the Error?

Dear Math Students, My teacher
gave me this problem:

Luther had 11 sheets of colored paper. 6 were
orange, and the rest were blue. Today he used
2 sheets of blue paper. How many sheets of
blue paper does Luther have now?

Here is what I did: $11 - 6 = 5$
Luther now has 5 blue sheets.

Is my answer correct? If not, please correct
my work and tell me what I did wrong.

Your friend,
Puzzled Penguin

1. Write an answer to Puzzled Penguin.

_____

▶ Solve Two Step Word Problems

Solve each problem. Label your answers.

2. The Hillside bus had
14 passengers. When it stopped,
5 people got off and 8 people got
on. How many people are riding
the Hillside bus now?

_____

3. There are 15 fish in a tank.
12 are goldfish, and the others
are angelfish. How many
more goldfish are there than
angelfish?

_____

▶ Solve and Discuss

Solve each problem. Label your answers.

4. Sun Mi picked 14 apricots. Celia picked 5 fewer apricots than Sun Mi. How many apricots did Sun Mi and Celia pick altogether?

5. Annie took 8 photographs at home and 7 photographs at school. Her sister Amanda took 6 fewer photographs than Annie. How many photographs did Amanda take?

6. There are 5 mice, 3 gerbils, and some hamsters in a cage. Altogether there are 15 animals in the cage. How many hamsters are there?

7. A new library opened on Saturday. The library lent out 234 books on Saturday. On Sunday, they lent out 138 books. That day, 78 books were returned. How many books were not returned?

8. Katie had 8 dimes and some nickels in her duck bank. She had 4 more nickels than dimes. She took out 5 nickels to buy a newspaper. How many nickels are in her duck bank now?

9. Tony had 14 colored pencils. 9 of them needed sharpening, and the rest were sharp. Yesterday, his uncle gave him some new colored pencils. Now Tony has 12 sharp colored pencils. How many colored pencils did his uncle give him?

▶ Is the Answer Reasonable?

Use rounding or mental math to decide if the answer is reasonable. Write *yes* or *no*. Then write an equation and solve the problem to see if you were correct.

Show your work.

10. Chelsea's class collected cans of food for their local food pantry. They collected 27 cans on Monday and 78 cans on Tuesday. Then on Wednesday they collected 53 cans. How many cans did the class collect on those three days?
Answer: 158 cans

_____

11. Barry strings beads. He had 54 beads on a string and he took off 29 beads. Then he took off 5 more. How many beads are on the string now?
Answer: 35 beads

_____

12. Dena counted the books on three shelves of the classroom library. She counted 33 books on the top shelf, 52 books on the middle shelf, and 48 books on the bottom shelf. How many books are on the three shelves?
Answer: 163 books

_____

13. Ms. Lance bought 6 packages of paper cups. Each package has 20 cups. She used 78 cups for a party. How many cups does Ms. Lance have left?
Answer: 58 cups

_____

© Houghton Mifflin Harcourt Publishing Company

▶ Reasonable Answers

Use rounding or mental math to decide if the answer is reasonable. Write *yes* or *no*. Then write an equation and solve the problem to see if you were correct.

Show your work.

14. There were 83 students in a spelling contest. In the first round 9 students were eliminated. Then 29 students were eliminated during the second round. How many students were left for the third round?
Answer: 24 students

_____

15. During one week Tina rode her bicycle 42 miles and Jim rode 9 fewer miles than Tina. How many miles did they ride altogether that week?
Answer: 75 miles

_____

16. Rusty volunteers at her local animal shelter. It costs $10 a day to care for a cat or dog in the shelter. The total cost to care for the animals one day was $90. There were 5 dogs at the shelter and the rest were cats. How many cats were at the shelter that day?
Answer: 9 cats

_____

17. Jake is saving money for a new bike that costs $187. He saved $55 one month and $44 the next month. How much more money does Jake need to buy the bike?
Answer: $88

_____

CA CC Content Standards **3.OA.3, 3.OA.8, 3.NBT.2**
Mathematical Practices **MP.1, MP.4**

Name _____   **Date** _____

► Equations and Two Step Word Problems

Write an equation and solve the problem.   *Show your work.*

1. Mrs. Delgado is baking pies and cakes for a school
   fundraiser. She bought 26 apples, 29 peaches, and
   a number of bananas at the Farmers' Market.
   She bought 66 pieces of fruit. How many bananas
   did she buy?

   _____

2. Abby bought 8 packages of stickers with the same
   number of stickers in each package. She gave
   15 stickers to her sister. Now Abby has 49 stickers.
   How many stickers were in each package?

   _____

3. Taylor is reading a 340-page book. He read 174 pages
   of the book on Saturday and 120 pages on Sunday.
   How many pages does he have left to read?

   _____

4. Lauren had a piece of ribbon that was 36 inches long.
   She cut a number of 3-inch pieces. She has 15 inches
   of ribbon left. How many 3-inch pieces did she cut?

   _____

5. There are 47 students in the marching band. There are
   5 students in the first row, and the rest are in equal
   rows of 6. How many students are in each of the 6 rows?

   _____

▶ Solve Two Step Word Problems

Write an equation and solve the problem.   *Show your work.*

6. Sara's mother baked 48 cookies. Sara gave a dozen cookies to her neighbor and divided the remaining cookies on plates of 9 cookies each. How many plates did she use?

   _____

7. Marissa is making floral bouquets. She bought 56 carnations, 73 chrysanthemums, and some roses. She bought 153 flowers in all. How many roses did she buy?

   _____

8. Thomas has 103 photos on his digital camera. He deletes 33 because they are out of focus. He wants to print the remaining photos and put an equal number on each page of an album that has 10 pages. How many photos will be on each page?

   _____

9. Leo bought 6 sets of books. Each set had the same number of books. He donated 11 books to the school library. Now he has 37 books left. How many books were in each set of books Leo bought?

   _____

10. Amber has 5 packages of chalk. Each package has 9 pieces of chalk. She gave a number of pieces of chalk to her brother. Amber has 37 pieces of chalk left. How many pieces did Amber give her brother?

    _____

► Write Two Step Equations

Write an equation and solve the problem.

Show your work.

1. Carrie sold 7 toys for 50¢ each and 1 toy for 75¢. How much money, in cents, did Carrie make?

_____

2. Darin earns $8 each week doing chores. He is saving his money to buy a game that costs $49 and a cap that costs $15. How many weeks will Darin need to save his money?

_____

3. A dog trainer is working with 7 dogs. He rewards each dog with the same number of treats. He started with 35 treats and he has 7 left. How many treats did he give each dog?

_____

4. Sheila has two dogs. One dog weighs 46 pounds and her other dog weighs 14 pounds more. How many pounds do the two dogs weigh altogether?

_____

5. Eli has 36 stamps and his brother has 24 stamps. They put their stamps in the same book. They put the same number of stamps on each page. They used 10 pages. How many stamps are on each page?

_____

► Write Two Step Equations (continued)

Write an equation and solve the problem.

Show your work.

6. There were 9 rows of chairs set up in the school gym. Each row had 20 chairs. After the students were seated, there were 12 empty chairs. How many chairs were filled?

_____

7. Eric had 143 baseball cards. His uncle gave him a number more. Then Eric gave 26 cards to a friend. He has 184 cards now. How many cards did Eric's uncle give him?

_____

8. Brandi had 8 equal rows of stickers. She bought 5 more and now she has 53 stickers. How many were in each row before she bought more?

_____

9. Randall cut a board into two pieces. One piece has a length of 84 inches. The other piece is 24 inches shorter. How long was the board Randall cut?

_____

10. A science poster shows 9 insects with 6 legs each and a spider with 8 legs. How many legs is that altogether?

_____

► Math and News

Little League Baseball Championships:
Wheaton Wolves Score Win

Wheaton Wolves win Little
League World Series Championship.
The chart shows some statistics from
the six games the team played.

Wheaton Wolves Statistics	
Times at Bat	155
Hits	47
Base on Balls	25
Runs Scored	36
Strike Outs	36

**Use the information in the table to write an equation
and solve the problem.**

1. How many times at bat did players not strike
   out or get a base on balls?

   _____

2. How many hits and base on balls did not result
   in a run?

   _____

3. The Wheaton Wolves had 13 triple or double-base
   hits, 3 homeruns, and the rest were single-base hits.
   How many single-base hits did the team get?

   _____

▶ Sports News

Danielle plays on a third grade basketball team in a league. Her team made the news when they scored 47 points, 41 points, and 53 points in a three-game tournament.

Write a two step equation and solve the problem.

4. How many points did Danielle's team score altogether?

_____

5. Describe a method you could use to decide if your answer to Problem 4 is reasonable.

_____

_____

_____

6. Danielle's scorecard shows her statistics for the three games. Use the information in the table to write equations to find the unknown numbers. Then complete the table.

_____

_____

	Number of 1-pt Free Throws	Number of 2-pt Field Goals	Total Points
Game 1	5	7	
Game 2		6	18
Game 3	3		21

Focus on Mathematical Practices

1. Mr. Taylor arranges some chairs in rows. He puts the same number of chairs in each of 7 rows and puts 7 chairs in the last row. He sets up 70 chairs. How many chairs does he put in each of the 7 equal rows?

   Choose the equation that can be used to solve the problem.

   I can use the equation
   | $(7 \times c) + 7 = 70$ |
   | $(70 \div 7) + 7 = c$ |
   | $(7 \times c) - 7 = 70$ |

   Solve the problem.

   _____ chairs

2. Marisol picks 150 flowers. She picks 80 red flowers and the rest are yellow. She sells 45 yellow flowers. How many yellow flowers does she have now?

   For numbers 2a–2e, choose Yes or No to tell whether the equation can be used to find the number of yellow flowers Marisol has now.

   2a. $150 - 80 - 45 = y$ ○ Yes   ○ No

   2b. $150 + 80 - 45 = y$ ○ Yes   ○ No

   2c. $150 + 80 + 45 = y$ ○ Yes   ○ No

   2d. $150 = 80 + 45 + y$ ○ Yes   ○ No

   2e. $150 = 80 - 45 + y$ ○ Yes   ○ No

3. Mark makes 18 picture frames this month. He makes 7 fewer picture frames than Sara. How many picture frames does Sara make?

Draw comparison bars to represent the problem. Then solve.

_____ picture frames.

4. David and Marne pick cucumbers at a farm. David picks 93 cucumbers. How many cucumbers does Marne pick?

What information is not helpful for solving the problem?

Ⓐ how many more cucumbers David picks

Ⓑ how many fewer cucumbers Marne picks

Ⓒ how many cucumbers are grown at the farm each year

Ⓓ how many cucumbers David and Marne pick

Rewrite the problem to include the necessary information. Then solve it.

5. There are 240 boys and girls in a soccer league. There are 130 girls. How many boys are there?

Write an equation with a variable to represent the problem. Then draw a Math Mountain to solve the problem.

_____ boys

6. On Wednesday, Jonah sees 30 birds and 4 rabbits. Of the birds, 13 are robins and the rest are pigeons. On Thursday, he sees some more pigeons. He has now seen 21 pigeons. How many pigeons did he see on Thursday?

Part A

Write the information in the correct box.

30 birds   4 rabbits   13 robins   21 pigeons

Needed Information	Extra Information

Part B

Solve the problem. What strategy did you use? How did it help?

7. Susan buys 24 postcards. She sends 6 postcards to friends. She puts the rest in 3 folders, with an equal number in each folder. How many postcards are in each folder?

Write the first step question and answer. Then solve.

_____ postcards

8. Kato uses 56 photos to make online albums. He puts 7 photos in each album. How many albums does Kato make?

For numbers 8a–8d, select True or False if the equation can be used to solve the problem.

8a. $7 \times a = 56$ ○ True   ○ False

8b. $56 \div 7 = a$ ○ True   ○ False

8c. $7 \times 56 = a$ ○ True   ○ False

8d. $56 \div a = 7$ ○ True   ○ False

9. Tara posts 35 flyers for the school carnival. Keisha posts 8 more flyers than Tara. How many flyers did Tara and Keisha post? Choose the number that completes the sentence.

Tara and Keisha post
| 43 |
| 62 |
| 78 |
flyers.

10. Jason packs 54 grapefruit in 9 boxes for shipping. He packs the same number of grapefruit in each box. How many grapefruit does Jason pack into each box?

Use the numbers and symbols to write a situation equation and a solution equation. Then solve.

| g | 9 | 54 | × | ÷ | = |

Situation Equation: _____

Solution Equation: _____

_____ grapefruit

11. Declan reads 19 books. He reads 13 fewer books than Ellie. How many books does Ellie read?

_____ books

12. Parker has 452 toy dinosaurs in his collection. His sister gives him 38 more toy dinosaurs. Then he sells some of them online. Parker now has 418 toy dinosaurs. How many did he sell?

Answer: 72 toy dinosaurs

Is the answer reasonable? Tell why or why not. Then write an equation and solve the problem.

13. Eva buys some items at the store and pays with pennies and nickels. Use the information in the table to write equations to find the unknown numbers. Then complete the table.

Pencil: _____

Eraser: _____

Clip: _____

	Number of Pennies	Number of Nickels	Total Cost
Pencil	6	8	¢
Eraser		4	24¢
Clip	2		37¢

14. Holly is going to the beach in 2 weeks and 4 days.

Which equation can be used to find the number of days until Holly goes to the beach?

Ⓐ $2 \times 7 + 4 = b$; $b = 18$ days

Ⓑ $2 \times 5 + 4 = b$; $b = 14$ days

Ⓒ $2 + 7 + 4 = b$; $b = 13$ days

Ⓓ $2 \times 7 - 4 = b$; $b = 10$ days

15. Omar has 5 ties and Ryan has 12 ties. How many more ties does Ryan have than Omar?

Make a comparison drawing to represent the problem. Then solve.

_____ more ties

Name _____ **Date** _____

CA CC Content Standards **3.G.1, 3.G.2**
Mathematical Practices **MP.2, MP.5, MP.7**

> **VOCABULARY**
> ray
> angle
> right angle

▶ Types of Angles

A **ray** is part of a line that has one endpoint and
continues forever in one direction. To draw
a ray, make an arrow to show that it goes on forever.

Two line segments or two rays that meet at
an endpoint form an **angle**.

An angle that forms a square corner is
called a **right angle**.

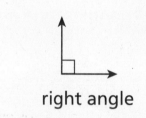
right angle

Some angles are smaller than a right angle.

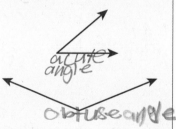
acute
angle

Some angles are larger than a right angle.

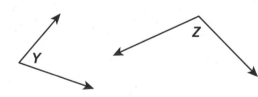
obtuse angle

These angles are named with a letter in the corner.

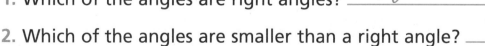

V   W   X   Y   Z

1. Which of the angles are right angles? _____ W

2. Which of the angles are smaller than a right angle? _____ X Y

3. Which of the angles are larger than a right angle? _____ Z V

VOCABULARY
triangle

▶ Describe Triangles by Types of Angles

Triangles can be described by the types of angles they have.

In these triangles, one angle is a right angle.

 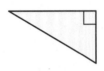 

In these triangles, three angles are smaller than a right angle.

In these triangles, one angle is larger than a right angle.

   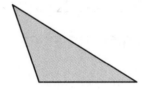

Use triangles K, L, and M for Exercises 4–6.

 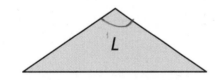 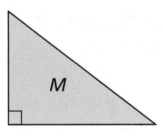

4. Which triangle has one right angle?

5. Which triangle has three angles smaller than a right angle?

K

6. Which triangle has one angle larger than a right angle?

▶ Describe Triangles by the Number of Sides of Equal Length

You can also describe triangles by the number of sides that are of equal length.

In these triangles, three sides are equal in length.

In these triangles, two sides are equal in length.

 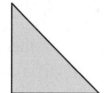 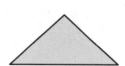

In these triangles, no sides are equal in length.

  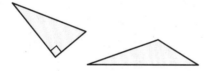

Use triangles _B_, _C_, and _D_ for Exercises 7–9.

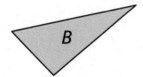

7. Which triangle has 3 sides of equal length?

_____

8. Which triangle has 2 sides of equal length?

_____

9. Which triangle has 0 sides of equal length?

_____

► **Describe Triangles by Types of Angles and Number of Sides of Equal Length**

Use triangles *M*, *N*, and *O* for 10–12. Write *M*, *N*, or *O*. Then complete the sentences.

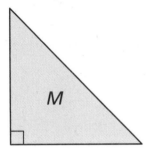

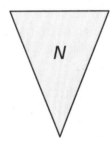

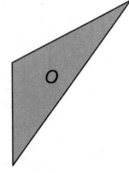

10. Triangle _____ has 1 angle larger than a right angle and has _____ sides of equal length.

11. Triangle _____ has 1 right angle and has _____ sides of equal length.

12. Triangle _____ has 3 angles smaller than a right angle and has _____ sides of equal length.

Use triangles *P*, *Q*, and *R* for 13–15. Write *P*, *Q*, or *R*. Then complete the sentences.

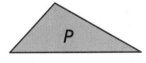

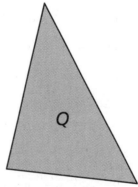

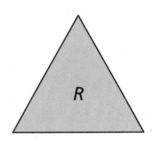

13. Triangle _____ has 3 angles smaller than a right angle and has _____ sides of equal length.

14. Triangle _____ has 3 angles smaller than a right angle and has _____ sides of equal length.

15. Triangle _____ has 1 angle larger than a right angle and has _____ sides of equal length.

Triangles

VOCABULARY
quadrilateral

▶ Build Quadrilaterals from Triangles

A **quadrilateral** is a figure with 4 sides.

Cut out each pair of triangles. Use each pair to make as many different quadrilaterals as you can. You may flip a triangle and use the back. On a separate piece of paper, trace each quadrilateral that you make.

Triangles with One Angle Larger Than a Right Angle

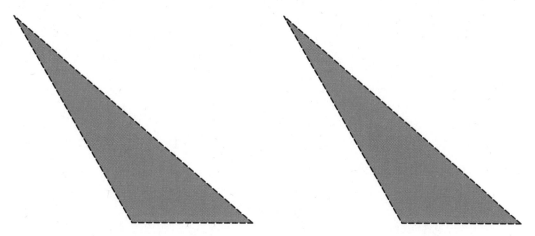

Triangles with Three Angles Smaller Than a Right Angle

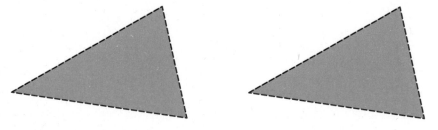

Triangles with One Right Angle

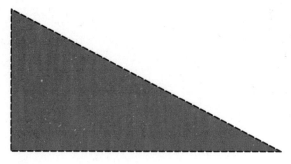
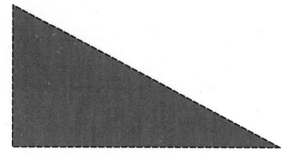

© Houghton Mifflin Harcourt Publishing Company

Triangles

VOCABULARY
polygon
concave
convex

► Polygons

A **polygon** is a flat, closed figure made up of line segments that do not cross each other.

Circle the figures that are polygons.

16. 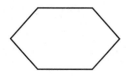   17.    18. 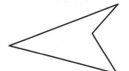   19.

20. 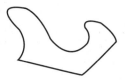   21. 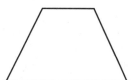   22.    23.

A figure can be **concave** or **convex**. In concave polygons, there exists a line segment with endpoints inside the polygon and a point on the line segment that is outside the polygon. A convex figure has no such line segment.

concave   convex

Which figures are convex and which are concave?

24. 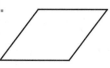   25.   26.    27.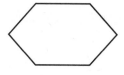

VOCABULARY
pentagon   hexagon
octagon   decagon

► Name Polygons

Polygons are named according to how many sides they have.

3 sides – **tri**angle   4 sides – **quad**rilateral   5 sides – **penta**gon

6 sides – **hexa**gon   8 sides – **octa**gon   10 sides – **deca**gon

Name each figure.

28.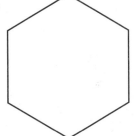

_____

29.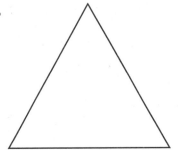

_____

30.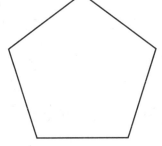

_____

31.

_____

32.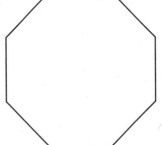

_____

33.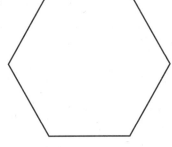

_____

34.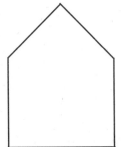

_____

35.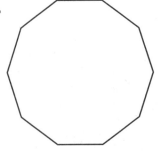

_____

36.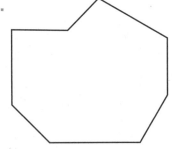

_____

► Build Polygons from Triangles

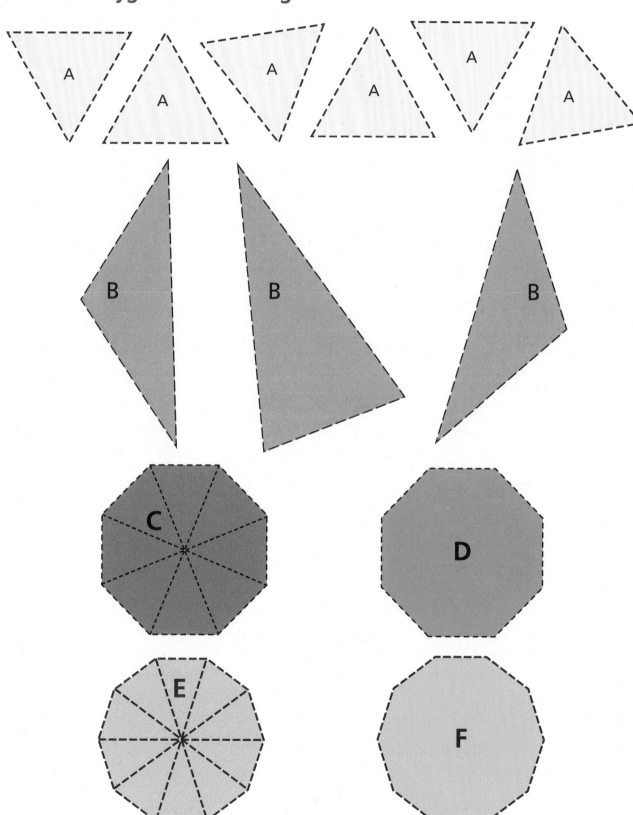

VOCABULARY
parallelogram

► Describe Parallelograms

All of these figures are **parallelograms**.

  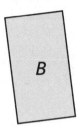 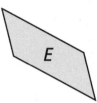

These figures are not parallelograms.

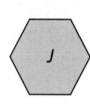  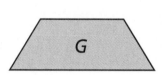 

Complete the sentence.

1. A parallelogram is a quadrilateral with _____

_____

► Measure Sides of Parallelograms

**For each parallelogram, measure the sides to the
nearest cm and label them with their lengths.**

2.

3.

4.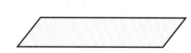

5. Look at the lengths of the sides. What patterns do
   you notice? _____

_____

VOCABULARY
rectangle
square
rhombus

► Describe Rectangles

All of these figures are **rectangles**.

Adel said, "Rectangles are special kinds of parallelograms."

Complete the sentence.

6. A rectangle is a parallelogram with _____

_____

► Explore Squares and Rhombuses

These figures are **squares**.   These figures are **rhombuses**.

Takeshi said, "Squares are special kinds of rectangles."

Cora said, "Rhombuses are special kinds of parallelograms."

Complete the sentence.

7. A square is a rectangle with _____

_____

8. A rhombus is a parallelogram with _____

_____

▶ Describe Quadrilaterals

Use as many words below as possible to describe each figure.

quadrilateral	parallelogram	rectangle	square

9.

_____

_____

_____

_____

10.

_____

_____

_____

_____

_____

11.

_____

_____

_____

_____

12.

_____

_____

_____

_____

VOCABULARY
trapezoid
opposite sides

► Describe Trapezoids

The quadrilaterals below are **trapezoids**.

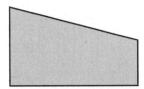

13. Write what you know about the **opposite sides** of a trapezoid.

_____

_____

14. Circle the quadrilaterals that are trapezoids.

 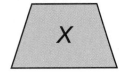 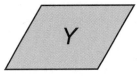 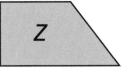

15. Explain why the figures you did not circle are not trapezoids.

_____

_____

_____

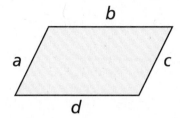

▶ **Draw Parallelograms**

1. Write what you know about the opposite sides of a parallelogram.

_____

_____

2. Draw three different parallelograms.

VOCABULARY
adjacent sides

▶ **Draw Rectangles**

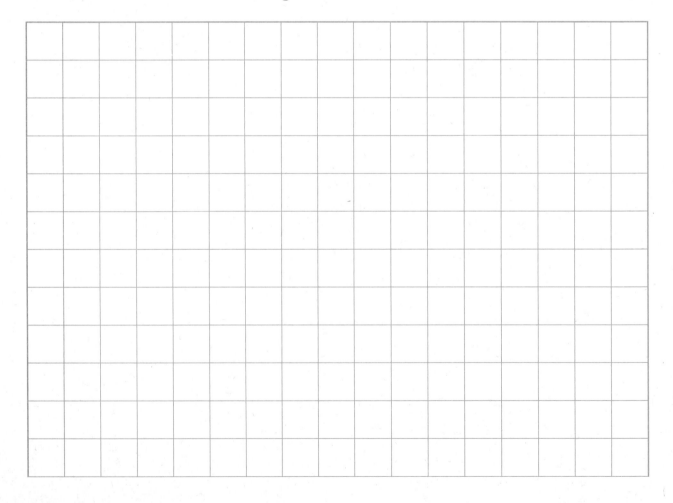

3. Write everything you know about the opposite sides
of a rectangle.

_____

4. What do you know about the **adjacent sides**
of a rectangle?

_____

5. Draw three different rectangles.

▶ Draw Squares and Rhombuses

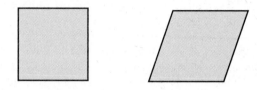

6. Write everything you know about squares.

_____

7. Write all you know about rhombuses.

_____

8. Draw two different squares and two different rhombuses.

▶ Draw Quadrilaterals That Are Not Squares, Rectangles, or Rhombuses

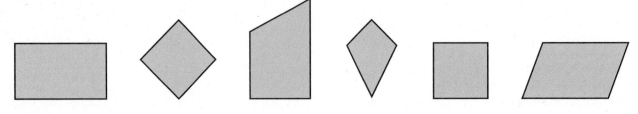

9. What is a quadrilateral?

_____

10. Name all the quadrilaterals that have at least one pair of parallel sides.

_____

11. Draw three different quadrilaterals that are not squares, rectangles, or rhombuses.

► Name Quadrilaterals

Place a check mark beside every name that describes the figure.

1.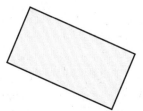

- [ ] quadrilateral
- [ ] parallelogram
- [ ] rhombus
- [ ] rectangle
- [ ] square

2.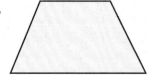

- [ ] quadrilateral
- [ ] parallelogram
- [ ] rhombus
- [ ] rectangle
- [ ] trapezoid

3.

- [ ] quadrilateral
- [ ] parallelogram
- [ ] rhombus
- [ ] rectangle
- [ ] square

4.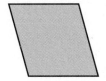

- [ ] quadrilateral
- [ ] parallelogram
- [ ] rhombus
- [ ] rectangle
- [ ] square

5.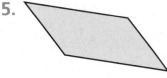

- [ ] quadrilateral
- [ ] parallelogram
- [ ] rhombus
- [ ] rectangle
- [ ] square

6.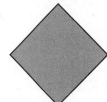

- [ ] quadrilateral
- [ ] parallelogram
- [ ] rhombus
- [ ] rectangle
- [ ] square

7.

- [ ] quadrilateral
- [ ] parallelogram
- [ ] rhombus
- [ ] rectangle
- [ ] square

8.

- [ ] quadrilateral
- [ ] parallelogram
- [ ] rhombus
- [ ] rectangle
- [ ] square

9.

- [ ] quadrilateral
- [ ] parallelogram
- [ ] rhombus
- [ ] rectangle
- [ ] square

▶ Analyze Quadrilaterals

10. For each figure, put Xs under the descriptions that are always true.

	Four sides	Both pairs of opposite sides parallel	Both pairs of opposite sides the same length	Four right angles	All sides the same length
Quadrilateral					
Trapezoid					
Parallelogram					
Rhombus					
Rectangle					
Square					

Use the finished chart above to complete each statement.

11. Parallelograms have all the features of quadrilaterals *plus*

_____

_____

12. Rectangles have all the features of parallelograms *plus*

_____

13. Squares have all the features of quadrilaterals *plus*

_____

_____

14. Trapezoids have all the features of quadrilaterals *plus*

_____

▶ Draw Quadrilaterals from a Description

Draw each figure.

15. Draw a quadrilateral that is *not* a parallelogram.

16. Draw a parallelogram that is *not* a rectangle.

17. Draw a rectangle that is *not* a square.

▶ What's the Error?

Dear Math Students,

Today I had to draw a quadrilateral with parallel sides that is not a rectangle, square, or rhombus. This is my drawing.

Is my drawing correct? If not, please help me understand why it is wrong.

Your friend,
Puzzled Penguin

18. Write an answer to Puzzled Penguin.

_____

_____

► Sort and Classify Quadrilaterals

Use the category diagram to sort the figures you cut out from Student Book page 333A. Write the letter of the figure in the diagram to record your work.

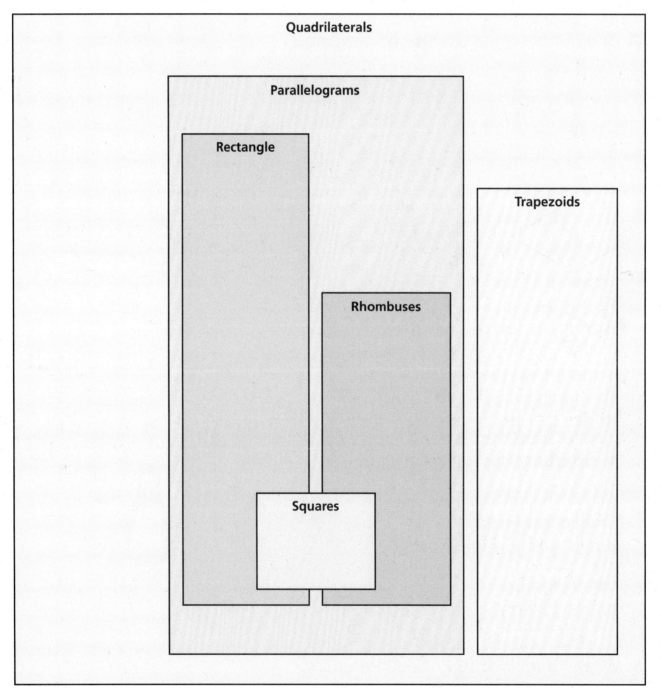

Classify Quadrilaterals

▶ Quadrilaterals for Sorting

Cut along the dashed lines.

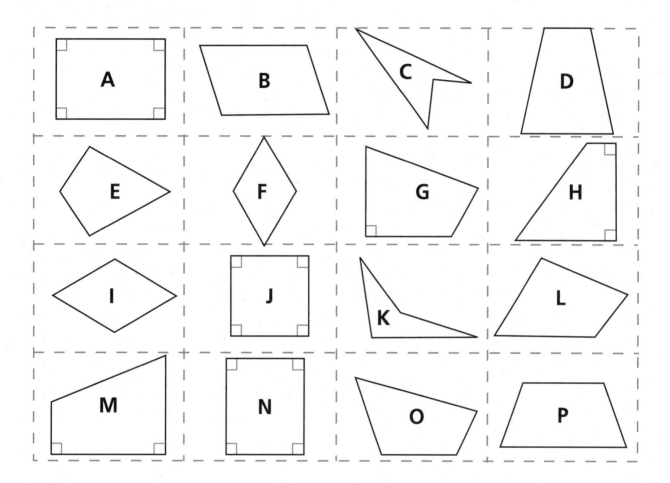

Family Letter

Content Overview

Dear Family,

Your child is currently learning about perimeter and area. Students begin to investigate the area of a rectangle by counting the number of square units inside the figure. Students also find the perimeter of a rectangle by counting linear units around the outside of the figure.

Students develop methods to find the perimeter and area of a rectangle, as shown below.

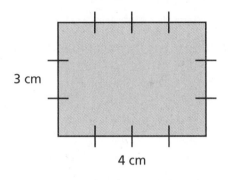

Perimeter = distance around the rectangle

Perimeter = side length + side length + side length + side length

$P = 4 \text{ cm} + 3 \text{ cm} + 4 \text{ cm} + 3 \text{ cm}$

$P = 14 \text{ cm}$

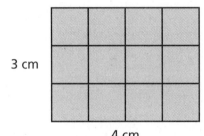

Area = square units inside the rectangle

Area = side length × side length

$A = 4 \text{ cm} \times 3 \text{ cm}$

$A = 12 \text{ sq cm}$

Students draw rectangles that have the same perimeter but different areas and rectangles that have the same area but different perimeters. They discover relationships between perimeter and area, such as that for a given area, the longest, skinniest rectangle has the greatest perimeter and the rectangle with sides closest to the same length or the same length has the least perimeter.

Students create shapes with tangrams, explore area relationships among the tangram shapes, and use the shapes as improvised units to measure area.

Throughout the unit students apply what they have learned about perimeter and area to real world problems.

If you have any questions or comments, please call or write to me.

Thank you.

Sincerely,
Your child's teacher

 CA CC

Unit 6 addresses the following standards from the *Common Core State Standards for Mathematics with California Additions*: 3.G.1, 3.G.2, 3.MD.5, 3.MD.5a, 3.MD.5b, 3.MD.6, 3.MD.7, 3.MD.7a, 3.MD.7b, 3.MD.7c, 3.MD.7d, 3.MD.8, and all Mathematical Practices.

Un vistazo general al contenido

Estimada familia:

Su niño está aprendiendo acerca de perímetro y área. Los estudiantes comenzarán a investigar el área de un rectángulo contando las unidades cuadradas que caben en la figura. También hallarán el perímetro de un rectángulo contando las unidades lineales alrededor de la figura.

Los estudiantes desarrollarán métodos para hallar el perímetro y el área de un rectángulo, como se muestra a continuación.

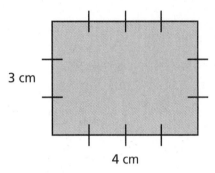

Perímetro = distancia alrededor del rectángulo

Perímetro = largo del lado + largo del lado + largo del lado + largo del lado

$P = 4 \text{ cm} + 3 \text{ cm} + 4 \text{ cm} + 3 \text{ cm}$

$P = 14 \text{ cm}$

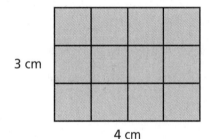

Área = unidades cuadradas dentro del rectángulo

Área = largo del lado × largo del lado

$A = 4 \text{ cm} \times 3 \text{ cm}$

$A = 12 \text{ cm cuad}$

Los estudiantes dibujarán rectángulos con el mismo perímetro pero diferentes áreas y rectángulos con la misma área pero diferentes perímetros. Descubrirán cómo se relacionan el perímetro y el área, por ejemplo, para un área determinada, el rectángulo más largo y angosto tiene el perímetro mayor y el rectángulo con lados de igual o casi igual longitud, tiene el perímetro menor.

Los estudiantes crearán figuras con tangramas, explorarán la relación entre el área de esas figuras y las usarán como medidas improvisadas para medir área.

Durante esta unidad los estudiantes aplicarán a problemas cotidianos lo que han aprendido acerca del perímetro y el área.

Si tiene alguna duda o algún comentario, por favor comuníquese conmigo.

Atentamente,
El maestro de su niño

 CA CC

En la Unidad 6 se aplican los siguientes estándares auxiliares, contenidos en los *Estándares estatales comunes de matemáticas con adiciones para California*: 3.G.1, 3.G.2, 3.MD.5, 3.MD.5a, 3.MD.5b, 3.MD.6, 3.MD.7, 3.MD.7a, 3.MD.7b, 3.MD.7c, 3.MD.7d, 3.MD.8 y todos los de prácticas matemáticas.

Perimeter and Area

CA CC Content Standards 3.MD.5, 3.MD.5a, 3.MD.5b, 3.MD.6, 3.MD.7, 3.MD.7a, 3.MD.7b, 3.MD.8
Mathematical Practices MP.2, MP.5

► Recognize Perimeter and Area

On this page, the dots on the dot paper are 1 cm apart. Use the rectangle for Exercises 1–4.

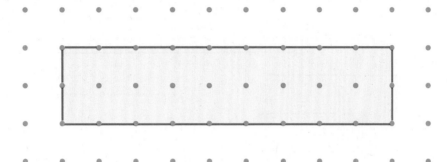

1. What part of the rectangle is its **perimeter**?

   _____

2. What part of the rectangle is its **area**?

   _____

3. Find the perimeter. Draw tick marks to help.

   _____

4. Find the area. Draw **unit squares** to help.

   _____

5. Draw a rectangle 5 cm long and 3 cm wide on the dot paper. Find the perimeter and area.

   Perimeter _____

   Area _____

6. Explain how you found the area of the rectangle in Exercise 5.

   _____

   _____

   _____

   _____

▶ Find Perimeter and Area

Find the perimeter and area of each figure.
Remember to include the correct units in your answers.

7. perimeter   area

1 sq cm

├─1 cm─┤

Perimeter = _____

Area = _____

8.

Perimeter = _____

Area = _____

9.

Perimeter = _____

Area = _____

10.

Perimeter = _____

Area = _____

11.

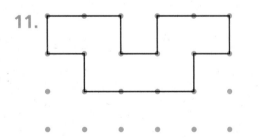

Perimeter = _____

Area = _____

12.

Perimeter = _____

Area = _____

Perimeter and Area

▶ Tile a Rectangle

Cut out the 1-inch unit squares along the dashed lines.
Try to cut as carefully and as straight as you can.

▶ Tile a Rectangle

13. Use the 1-inch unit squares from page 337A to cover the rectangle below.

14. Check whether there are any gaps between the unit squares.

_____

15. Check whether any unit squares overlap.

_____

16. Draw lines to show the unit squares. The number of unit squares is the area in square inches. What is the area?

_____

17. Use an inch ruler to measure the side lengths of the rectangle. Label the length and the width.

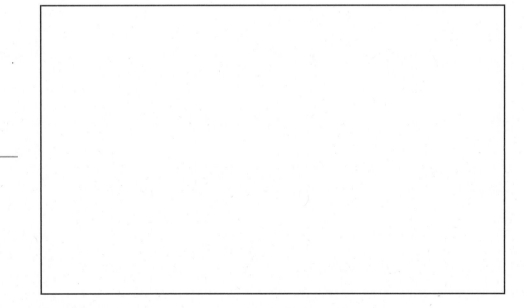

18. Write a multiplication equation to show the area.

_____

▶ Tile a Rectangle (continued)

**Cover each rectangle with 1-inch unit squares.
Count the squares to find the area. Then write
an equation to show the area.**

19.

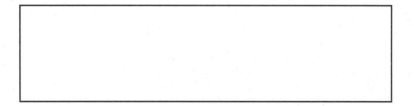

The area is _____   The equation is _____

20.

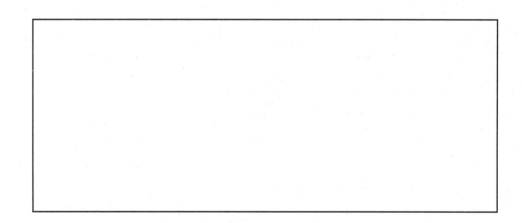

The area is _____   The equation is _____

21. How many 1-inch unit squares are needed to cover
a rectangle that is 7 inches long and 4 inches wide?

_____

22. What is the area of a rectangle that is 7 inches long
and 4 inches wide?

_____

Name _____ Date _____

CA CC Content Standards 3.MD.7, 3.MD.7b, 3.MD.7c, 3.MD.7d, 3.MD.8
Mathematical Practices MP.1, MP.2, MP.4

▶ Write Different Equations for Area

1. Use the drawings. Show two ways to find the area of a rectangle that is 10 units long and 6 units wide.

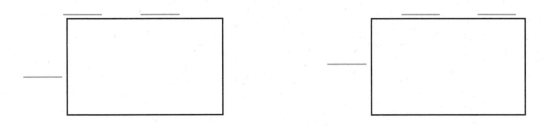

2. Write equations for your two rectangle drawings.

   _____   _____

3. Suppose the rectangle is 10 feet long and 6 feet wide. What is its area?

   _____

4. Suppose the rectangle is 10 meters long and 6 meters wide. What is its area?

   _____

5. Use drawings and write equations to show two ways to find the area of a rectangle that is 9 yards long and 5 yards wide.

   _____   _____

▶ Rectangle Equations and Drawings

Write an equation for each rectangle.

6.
```
        3   +    5
      ┌──────┬────────┐
    4 │      │        │
      └──────┴────────┘
```

_____

7.
```
       2  +  4
      ┌────┬────┐
      │    │    │
    5 │    │    │
      │    │    │
      └────┴────┘
```

_____

8.
```
        3   +     6
      ┌─────┬────────┐
    3 │     │        │
      └─────┴────────┘
```

_____

9.
```
        4   +    4
      ┌──────┬──────┐
      │      │      │
    4 │      │      │
      │      │      │
      └──────┴──────┘
```

_____

Draw a rectangle for each equation.

10. $(3 \times 3) + (3 \times 5) = 3 \times 8$

11. $(4 \times 5) + (4 \times 3) = 4 \times 8$

12. $(5 \times 3) + (5 \times 6) = 5 \times 9$

13. $(4 \times 6) + (4 \times 4) = 4 \times 10$

© Houghton Mifflin Harcourt Publishing Company

Side Lengths with Area and Perimeter

▶ Find Unknown Side Lengths

Find the unknown side length in each diagram.

14.

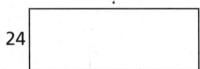

8 cm

?

Area = 72 sq cm

_____

15.

12 cm

?

Perimeter = 38 cm

_____

16.

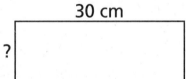

?

24

Perimeter = 64 cm

_____

17.

7 cm

?

Area = 56 sq cm

_____

18.

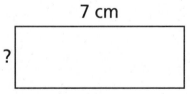

30 cm

?

Perimeter = 72 cm

_____

19.

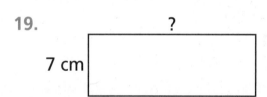

?

7 cm

Area = 63 sq cm

_____

20.

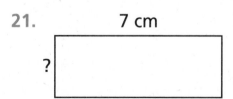

7 cm

?

Area = 28 sq cm

_____

21.

7 cm

?

Perimeter = 28 cm

_____

► Unknown Side Length Problems

Solve. Draw a rectangle to represent the situation.

Show your work.

22. Alexander and his grandfather are tiling their rectangular kitchen floor. They need to use 42 tiles. They are making rows of 7 tiles. How many rows do they make?

_____

23. Tilly and her mom made a rectangular dog run. They used 12 one-yard long pieces of fencing. They put 2 pieces of fencing on one side. How many pieces did they put on the next side?

_____

24. Martha is making a quilt. She has 63 squares ready to sew together. She wants the quilt to be 9 rows long. How many squares will be in each row?

_____

25. Rick and Roger are painting a mural made up of different sizes of rectangles, with no gaps or overlaps of the rectangles. They have enough paint to cover 15 square yards. They want the mural to be 3 yards long. How wide can the mural be?

_____

26. Mr. Baker wants to use all of a 48-inch strip of oak trim for a box he plans to make. He wants the box to be 14 inches wide. How long will the box be?

_____

Name _____ **Date** _____

CA CC Content Standards **3.MD.7b, 3.MD.8**
Mathematical Practices **MP.2, MP.8**

▶ Compare Rectangles with the Same Perimeter

Complete.

1. On a centimeter dot grid, draw all possible rectangles with a perimeter of 12 cm and sides whose lengths are whole centimeters. Label the lengths of two adjacent sides of each rectangle.

2. Find and label the area of each rectangle. In the table, record the lengths of the adjacent sides and the area of each rectangle.

3. Compare the shapes of the rectangles with the least and greatest areas.

Rectangles with Perimeter 12 cm	
Lengths of Two Adjacent Sides	Area

4. On a centimeter dot grid, draw all possible rectangles with a perimeter of 22 cm and sides whose lengths are whole centimeters. Label the lengths of two adjacent sides of each rectangle.

5. Find and label the area of each rectangle. In the table, record the lengths of the adjacent sides and the area of each rectangle.

Rectangles with Perimeter 22 cm	
Lengths of Two Adjacent Sides	Area

6. Compare the shapes of the rectangles with the least and greatest areas.

▶ Compare Rectangles with the Same Area

Complete.

7. On a centimeter dot grid, draw all possible rectangles with an area of 12 sq cm and sides whose lengths are whole centimeters. Label the lengths of two adjacent sides of each rectangle.

8. Find and label the perimeter of each rectangle. In the table, record the lengths of the adjacent sides and the perimeter of each rectangle.

Rectangles with Area 12 sq cm	
Lengths of Two Adjacent Sides	Perimeter

9. Compare the shapes of the rectangles with the least and greatest perimeter.

_____

_____

10. On a centimeter dot grid, draw all possible rectangles with an area of 18 sq cm and sides whose lengths are whole centimeters. Label the lengths of two adjacent sides of each rectangle.

11. Find and label the perimeter of each rectangle. In the table, record the lengths of the adjacent sides and the perimeter of each rectangle.

Rectangles with Area 18 sq cm	
Lengths of Two Adjacent Sides	Perimeter

12. Compare the shapes of the rectangles with the least and greatest perimeter.

_____

_____

▶ Find Area by Decomposing into Rectangles (continued)

Decompose each figure into rectangles.
Then find the area of the figure.

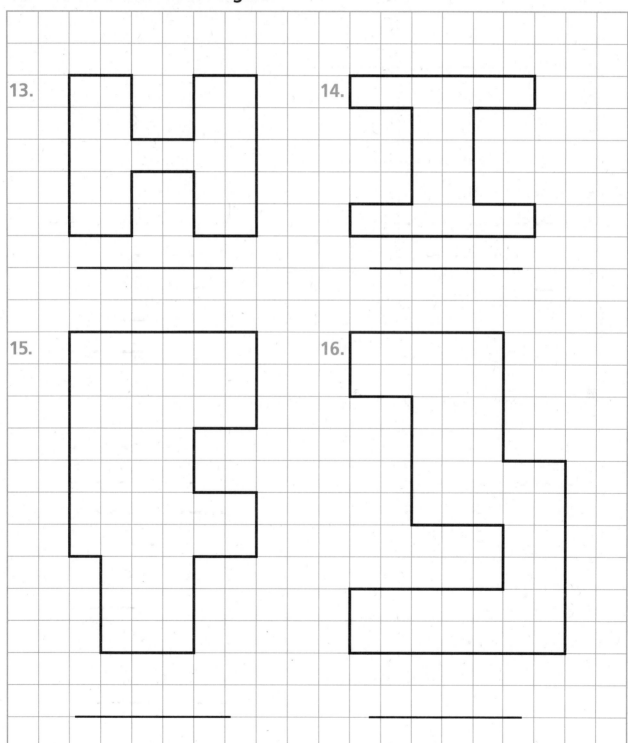

Name _____   **Date** _____

▶ **What's the Error?**

Dear Math Students,

Today my teacher asked me to find the area of a figure. I knew that I could decompose the figure into rectangles. This is what I did.

Rectangle 1

Rectangle 2

Area of Rectangle 1:
3 x 6 = 18 square units

Area of Rectangle 2:
5 x 4 = 20 square units

Area of Figure:
18 + 20 = 38 square units

Is my work correct? If not, please correct my work and tell me what I did wrong. How do you know my answer is wrong?

Your friend,
Puzzled Penguin

17. Write an answer to Puzzled Penguin.

_____

_____

_____

_____

Area of Rectilinear Figures

Name _____ Date _____

CA CC Content Standards **3.MD.7b, 3.MD.8**
Mathematical Practices **MP.1, MP.4**

► Solve Perimeter and Area Problems

Solve. Circle whether you need to find a perimeter, an area, or an unknown side length. Draw a diagram to represent each situation.

Show your work.

1. The dimensions of a rectangular picture frame are 9 inches and 6 inches. What is the area of a picture that would fit in the frame?

   Perimeter   Area   Side Length

   _____

2. A garden has the shape of a hexagon. Each side of the garden is 5 feet long. How much fence is needed to go around the garden?

   Perimeter   Area   Side Length

   _____

3. The length of a water slide is 9 yards. The slide is 2 yards wide. How much of the surface of the slide must be covered with water?

   Perimeter   Area   Side Length

   _____

4. Mr. Schmidt is installing 32 cubbies in the hallway. He puts 8 cubbies in each row. How many rows of cubbies can he make?

   Perimeter   Area   Side Length

   _____

► Solve Perimeter and Area Problems (continued)

Solve. Circle whether you need to find a perimeter, an area, or an unknown side length. Draw a diagram to represent each situation.

Show your work.

5. The floor of a delivery van has an area of 56 square feet and is 8 feet long. How many rows of 8 boxes that measure 1 foot by 1 foot can be put in the delivery van?

    Perimeter   Area   Side Length

    _____

6. Zack is planning to make a flower garden. He has 24 one-yard sections of fence that he plans to place around the garden. He wants the garden to be as long as possible. What is the longest length he can use for the garden? How wide will the garden be?

    Perimeter   Area   Side Length

    _____

7. A spa is 9 yards long and 7 yards wide. A locker room 8 yards long and 6 yards wide is at one end of the spa. How much floor space do the spa and the locker room take up?

    Perimeter   Area   Side Length

    _____

8. Rosa's dog Sparky is 24 inches long. One side of Sparky's doghouse is 36 inches long and the other side is twice as long as Sparky. What is the distance around Sparky's doghouse?

    Perimeter   Area   Side Length

    _____

▶ Solve Perimeter and Area Problems (continued)

Solve. Circle whether you need to find a perimeter, an area, or an unknown side length. Draw a diagram to represent each situation.

Show your work.

9. Joanne made 16 fruit bars in a square pan. The fruit bars are 2 inches by 2 inches. What are the dimensions of the pan she used to bake the fruit bars?

Perimeter   Area   Side Length

_____

10. A scout troop is making triangular pennants for their tents. Two sides of each pennant are 2 feet long and the third side is 1 foot long. How much binding tape is needed to go around 4 pennants?

Perimeter   Area   Side Length

_____

11. A rectangular quilt is 5 feet wide and 7 feet long. How many feet of lace are needed to cover the edges of the quilt?

Perimeter   Area   Side Length

_____

12. Amy has a piece of fleece fabric that is 4 feet wide and 6 feet long. How many squares of fleece fabric that are 1 foot wide and 1 foot long can she cut from the fabric?

Perimeter   Area   Side Length

_____

► Solve Perimeter and Area Problems (continued)

Solve. Circle whether you need to find a perimeter, an area, or an unknown side length. Draw a diagram to represent each situation.

Show your work.

13. Leighanne has 23 tiles with dimensions of 1 foot by 1 foot. She wants to tile a hallway that is 8 feet long and 3 feet wide. Does she have enough tiles? If not, how many more does she need?

    Perimeter   Area   Side Length

14. Mrs. Brown has 48 one-foot pieces of garden fence for her new vegetable garden. She wants to have as much room as possible to plant the vegetables. What dimensions should she use for the garden?

    Perimeter   Area   Side Length

15. Martha has 27 quilt patches with animals and 27 patches with flowers. She wants her quilt to have rows of 6 patches. How many rows will the quilt have?

    Perimeter   Area   Side Length

16. A park in the shape of a triangle has a 20-mile bike path going along the sides. Donald rode 6 miles on the first side and 8 miles on the second side. How long is the third side of the park?

    Perimeter   Area   Side Length

▶ Explore Tangrams

Cut one tangram figure into pieces along the dotted lines. Try to cut as carefully and as straight as you can. Save the other figures to use later.

► **Explore Tangrams (continued)**

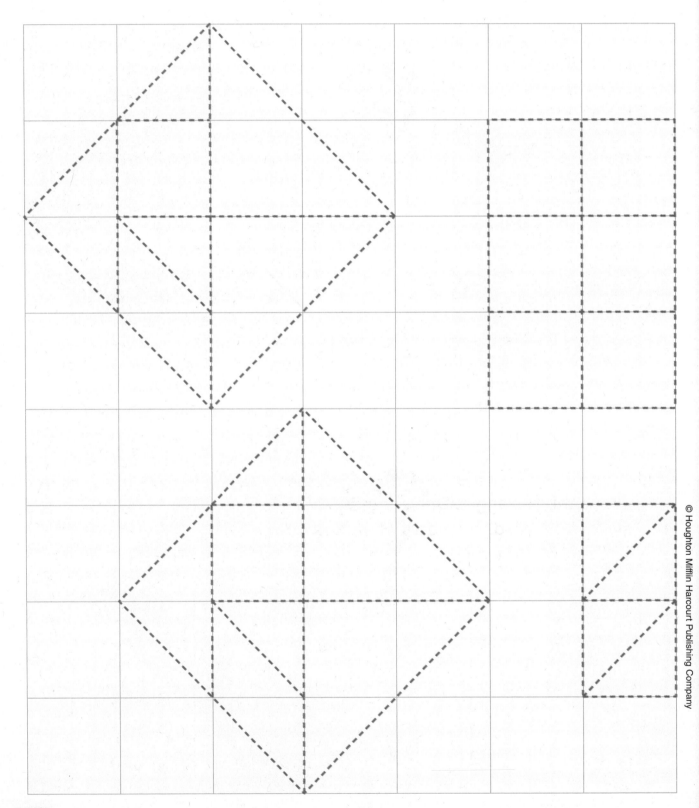

Tangram Shapes and Area

Name _____ **Date** _____

CA CC Content Standards **3.MD.6**
Mathematical Practices **MP.7**

▶ **Solve Tangram Puzzles**

Use the tangram pieces from page 353A.

1. Make this bird. When you finish, draw lines
   to show how you placed the pieces.

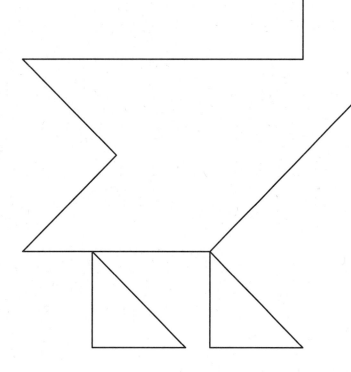

2. Make this rectangle. Draw lines to show
   how you placed the pieces. Hint: You do
   not need all the pieces.

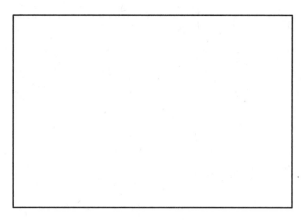

▶ Solve Tangram Puzzles (continued)

**Use the tangram pieces. Draw lines to show
how you placed the pieces.**

3. Make this boat.

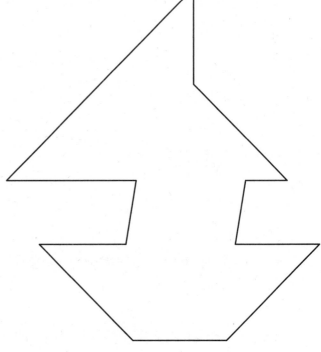

4. Make this tree.

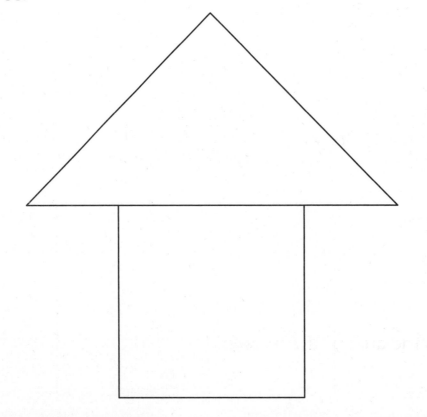

Tangram Shapes and Area

▶ Use Tangram Pieces to Find Area

5. Use the seven tangram pieces. Cover this rectangle.

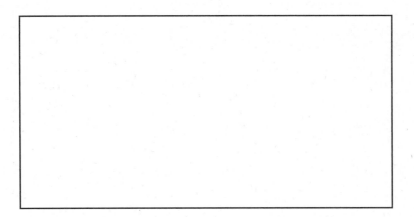

6. What is the area of the rectangle?

_____

7. Use any tangram pieces. Cover this rectangle.

8. What is the area of the rectangle?

_____

► Use Tangram Pieces to Find Area (continued)

Use any tangram pieces. Cover each rectangle.

9.

What is the area of the rectangle?

10.

What is the area of the square?

Tangram Shapes and Area

▶ Use Tangram Pieces to Find Area (continued)

Use any tangram pieces. Cover each figure.

11.

12.

What is the area of the square?

_____

What is the area of the rectangle?

_____

13.

What is the area of the figure?

_____

► Use Tangram Pieces to Find Area (continued)

Use any tangram pieces. Cover each figure.

14.

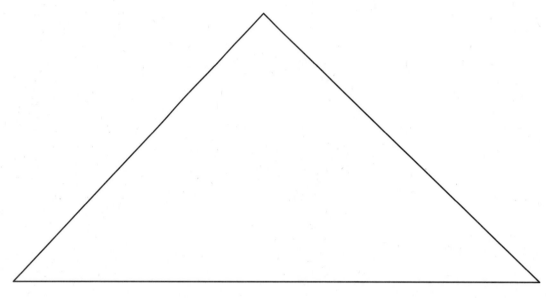

What is the area of the triangle?

_____

15.

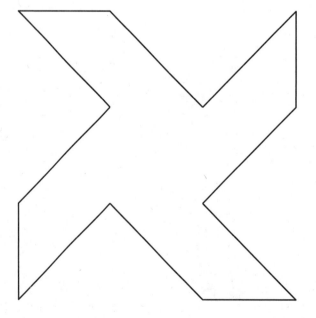

What is the area of the figure?

_____

Tangram Shapes and Area

Name

Date

CA CC Content Standards **3.MD.7d, 3.MD.8**
Mathematical Practices **MP.1, MP.2, MP.4**

▶ Math and Gardening

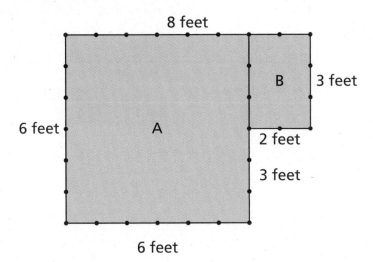

Look at the drawing of Yoakim's garden.
It is divided into two quadrilaterals.

1. What is the perimeter of part A? _____

   What is the perimeter of part B? _____

2. What is the perimeter of the combined
   garden? _____

3. Will Yoakim need more fencing to enclose the two
   parts of his garden separately or to enclose the
   combined garden?

   _____

4. What is the area of part A? _____

   What is the area of part B? _____

5. What is the area of the combined garden?

   _____

6. How does the total area of the two parts of the garden
   compare to the area of the combined garden?

   _____

► **Design a Garden**

Use the dot paper below to draw a different garden that has the same perimeter as Yoakim's combined garden. Beside it, draw a different garden that has the same area as Yoakim's garden.

|–1 ft–|

7. What is the area of your garden that has the same perimeter as Yoakim's garden?

_____

8. What is the perimeter of your garden that has the same area as Yoakim's garden?

_____

9. Use the centimeter dot paper at the right to draw separate areas within a garden where you would plant corn, beans, and tomatoes.

The area for corn is 12 square feet.
The area for beans is 25 square feet.
The area for tomatoes is 20 square feet.

Focus on Mathematical Practices

1. Write the letter for each shape in the box that describes the shape.

 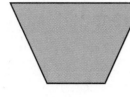  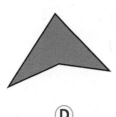

Ⓐ   Ⓑ   Ⓒ   Ⓓ

Quadrilateral	Parallelogram	Four right angles	All sides the same length

2. Draw two different parallelograms that are not squares or rhombuses.

How did you decide which figures to draw?

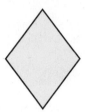
Name _____ Date _____

3. Emily draws this figure.

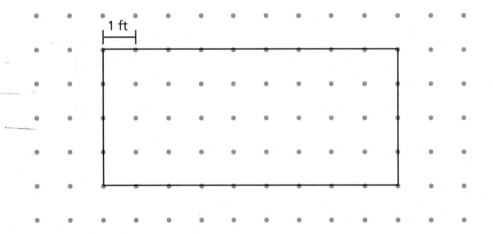

For numbers 3a–3e, choose Yes or No to tell whether the name describes the figure.

3a. quadrilateral   ○ Yes   ○ No

3b. rectangle   ○ Yes   ○ No

3c. parallelogram   ○ Yes   ○ No

3d. rhombus   ○ Yes   ○ No

3e. square   ○ Yes   ○ No

4. Mr. Gomez hangs a mural on the classroom wall. Find the perimeter and area of the mural.

1 ft

Perimeter: _____ feet

Area: _____ square feet

5. Liana plants a vegetable garden in two sections. She plants corn in a section that is 5 meters long and 6 meters wide. She plants squash in a section that is 3 meters long and 6 meters wide.

Part A
Describe one way to find the area of the garden. Then find the area.

Area: _____ square meters

Part B
Draw a picture of the garden to show your answer is correct.

6. A park ranger has 32 feet of fencing to fence four sides of a rectangular recycling site. What is the greatest area of recycling site that the ranger can fence? Explain how you know.

7. This hexagon has been divided into triangles with equal areas. What part of the area of the hexagon is the area of each triangle?

Ⓐ $\frac{1}{2}$

Ⓑ $\frac{1}{5}$

Ⓒ $\frac{1}{6}$

Ⓓ $\frac{6}{6}$

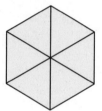

8. The octagon has been divided into triangles with equal areas. The area of each triangle is 2 square units.

Choose the number that completes the sentence.

The area of the octagon is
| 2 |
| 8 |
| 16 |
| 18 |
square units.

9. Steve makes a banner with an area of 8 square feet. On the grid, draw all possible rectangles with an area of 8 square feet and sides whose lengths are whole feet. Label the lengths of two adjacent sides of each rectangle. Label each rectangle with its perimeter.

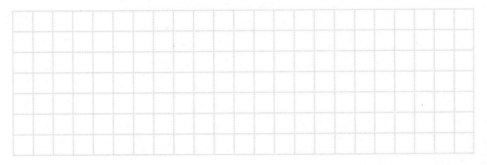

Compare the perimeters of the banners. What do you notice about their shapes?

10. Zack uses 64 inches of wood to build a rectangular picture frame. The length of one side is 25 inches. What is the length of the other side?

What do you need to find to solve the problem? Choose the word that completes the sentence.

I need to find the | area
perimeter
side length | of the picture frame.

_____

11. Hailey's patio is 9 feet long. If the area of the patio is 90 square feet, how wide is the patio?

_____ feet

12. Draw a line from the figure to the area of the figure.

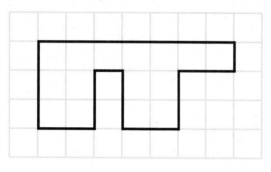

●   ● 13 square units

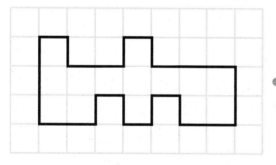

●   ● 14 square units

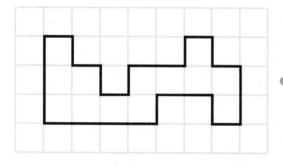

●   ● 15 square units

13. Riki cuts two decagons out of cardboard. Then he glues yarn around the edges. How much yarn does Riki use if each edge of the decagon is 8 centimeters?

_____ centimeters

14. Select all the figures that are quadrilaterals.

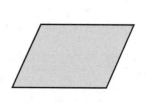

○   ○   ○   ○   ○

Family Letter

Content Overview

Dear Family,

In this unit, your child will be introduced to fractions. Students will build fractions from unit fractions and explore fractions as parts of a whole.

Unit Fraction

|← 1 whole →|

| $\frac{1}{3}$ | $\frac{1}{3}$ | $\frac{1}{3}$ |

$$\frac{1}{3} + \frac{1}{3} = \frac{2}{3}$$

Fraction of a Whole

$\frac{3}{4}$ ← numerator
← denominator

Students will find equivalent fractions, and compare fractions with either the same denominator or the same numerator.

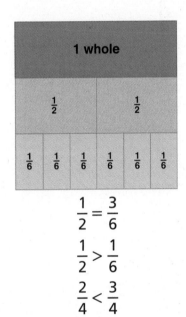

$$\frac{1}{2} = \frac{3}{6}$$

$$\frac{1}{2} > \frac{1}{6}$$

$$\frac{2}{4} < \frac{3}{4}$$

In this unit, your child will also solve real world problems using his or her understanding of fraction concepts.

Please call if you have any questions or comments.

Sincerely,
Your child's teacher

CA CC

Unit 7 addresses the following standards from the *Common Core State Standards for Mathematics with California Additions*: 3.NF.1, 3.NF.2, 3.NF.2a, 3.NF.2b, 3.NF.3, 3.NF.3a, 3.NF.3b, 3.NF.3c, 3.NF.3d, 3.G.2, and for all Mathematical Practices.

Carta a la familia

Un vistazo general al contenido

Estimada familia:

En esta unidad, se le presentarán por primera vez las fracciones a su niño. Los estudiantes formarán fracciones con fracciones unitarias y explorarán las fracciones como partes de un entero.

Fracción unitaria

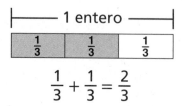

$$\frac{1}{3} + \frac{1}{3} = \frac{2}{3}$$

Fracción de un entero

$\frac{3}{4}$ ← numerador
← denominador

Los estudiantes hallarán fracciones equivalentes y compararán fracciones del mismo denominador o del mismo numerador.

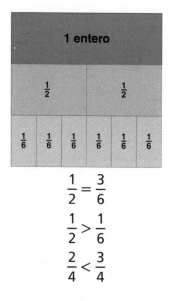

$$\frac{1}{2} = \frac{3}{6}$$

$$\frac{1}{2} > \frac{1}{6}$$

$$\frac{2}{4} < \frac{3}{4}$$

En esta unidad, su niño también resolverá problemas cotidianos usando los conceptos que aprenda sobre fracciones.

Si tiene alguna duda o algún comentario, por favor comuníquese conmigo.

Atentamente,
El maestro de su niño

© Houghton Mifflin Harcourt Publishing Company

 CA CC

En la Unidad 7 se aplican los siguientes estándares auxiliares, contenidos en los *Estándares estatales comunes de matemáticas con adiciones para California*: **3.NF.1, 3.NF.2, 3.NF.2a, 3.NF.2b, 3.NF.3, 3.NF.3a, 3.NF.3b, 3.NF.3c, 3.NF.3d, 3.G.2** y todos los de prácticas matemáticas.

Understand Fractions

► Fraction Rectangles

Cut out the bottom rectangle first.
Then cut on the dotted lines to make 4 rectangles.
Wait to cut out the top rectangle.

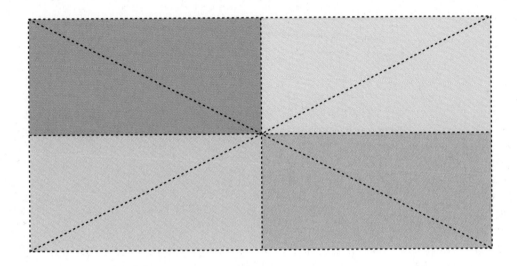

Name _____ **Date** _____

CA CC Content Standards **3.NF.1, 3.G.2**
Mathematical Practices **MP.2, MP.7**

► Explore Unit Fractions

Use your rectangles from page 369A to make the whole shape. Count the equal parts. What unit fraction of the whole shape is one of the rectangles?

1.

Number of equal parts _____   Unit fraction _____

2.

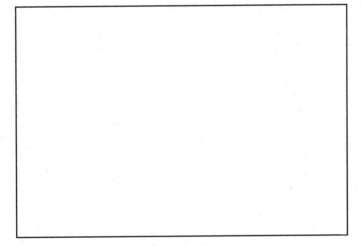

Number of equal parts _____   Unit fraction _____

3.

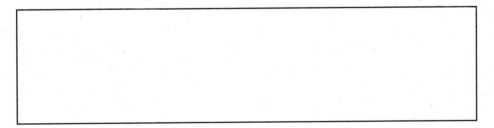

Number of equal parts _____   Unit fraction _____

▶ Explore Unit Fractions (continued)

Use your triangles from page 369A to make a whole shape like the model shown. Count the equal parts in the whole. What unit fraction of the whole shape is the blue triangle?

4.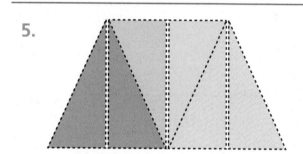

There are _____ equal parts in the whole shape.

The blue triangle is _____ of the whole shape.

5.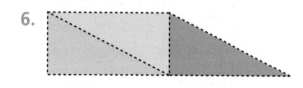

There are _____ equal parts in the whole shape.

The blue triangle is _____ of the whole shape.

6.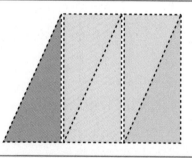

There are _____ equal parts in the whole shape.

The blue triangle is _____ of the whole shape.

7.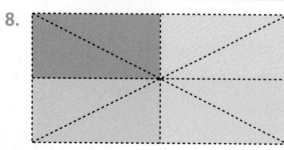

There are _____ equal parts in the whole shape.

The blue triangle is _____ of the whole shape.

8.

There are _____ equal parts in the whole shape.

One blue triangle is _____ of the whole shape.

Understand Fractions

▶ Unit Fractions and Fraction Bars

You can represent a **fraction** with a fraction bar. The **denominator** tells how many equal parts the whole is divided into. The **numerator** tells how many equal parts you are talking about.

1 whole

$\frac{1}{3}$ ← numerator
← denominator

Shade 1 part.

A **unit fraction** has a numerator of 1. Shade the rest of the fraction bars at the right below to represent unit fractions. What patterns do you see?

1 whole → Shade 1 whole.   1   one

Divide the whole into 2 equal parts. → Shade 1 part. $\frac{1}{2}$ one half

Divide the whole into 3 equal parts. → Shade 1 part. $\frac{1}{3}$ one third

Divide the whole into 4 equal parts. → Shade 1 part. $\frac{1}{4}$ one fourth

Divide the whole into 5 equal parts. → Shade 1 part. $\frac{1}{5}$ one fifth

Divide the whole into 6 equal parts. → Shade 1 part. $\frac{1}{6}$ one sixth

Divide the whole into 7 equal parts. → Shade 1 part. $\frac{1}{7}$ one seventh

Divide the whole into 8 equal parts. → Shade 1 part. $\frac{1}{8}$ one eighth

► Build Fractions from Unit Fractions

Write the unit fractions for each whole. Next, shade the correct number of parts. Then show each shaded fraction as a sum of unit fractions.

9. [bar divided into 5 parts] → [bar with 2 parts shaded] Shade 2 parts.

   Divide the whole into 5 equal parts.

   $\frac{1}{5} + \frac{1}{5} + \frac{1}{5} + \frac{1}{5} + \frac{1}{5}$ $\qquad$ $\frac{1}{5} + \frac{1}{5} = \frac{2}{5}$

10. [bar divided into 3 parts] → [bar divided into 3 parts] Shade 2 parts.

    Divide the whole into 3 equal parts.

    _____

11. [bar divided into 7 parts] → [bar divided into 7 parts] Shade 5 parts.

    Divide the whole into 7 equal parts.

    _____

12. [bar divided into 8 parts] → [bar divided into 8 parts] Shade 7 parts.

    Divide the whole into 8 equal parts.

    _____

13. [bar divided into 6 parts] → [bar divided into 6 parts] Shade 3 parts.

    Divide the whole into 6 equal parts.

    _____

14. [bar divided into 8 parts] → [bar divided into 8 parts] Shade 8 parts.

    Divide the whole into 8 equal parts.

    _____

Understand Fractions

Name _____ **Date** _____

CA CC Content Standards **3.NF.1, 3.G.2**
Mathematical Practices **MP.2, MP.7**

▶ Use Fraction Bars

Shade each fraction bar to show the fraction.
First, divide the fraction bar into the correct unit fractions.

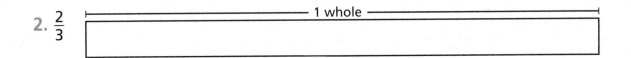

1. $\frac{1}{6}$

2. $\frac{2}{3}$

3. $\frac{7}{8}$

4. $\frac{2}{4}$

5. $\frac{5}{6}$

6. $\frac{3}{8}$

Name _____   Date _____

► **Use Number Lines**

Mark each number line to show the fraction.
First, divide the number line into the correct unit fractions.

7. $\frac{1}{6}$

8. $\frac{2}{3}$

9. $\frac{7}{8}$

10. $\frac{2}{4}$

11. $\frac{5}{6}$

12. $\frac{3}{8}$

Model Fractions

Name _____ Date _____

CA CC Content Standards **3.NF.2, 3.NF.2a, 3.NF.2b, 3.NF.3, 3.NF.3c**
Mathematical Practices **MP.2, MP.7**

► Locate Fractions Less Than 1

Locate each fraction on the number line.
Draw more number lines if you need to.

1. $\frac{1}{4}$ ← + |———————————————| + →
              0   1

2. $\frac{1}{8}$ ← + |———————————————| + →
              0   1

3. $\frac{2}{3}$ ← + |———————————————| + →
              0   1

4. $\frac{5}{6}$ ← + |———————————————| + →
              0   1

5. $\frac{1}{6}$ and $\frac{2}{3}$ ← + |———————————————| + →
                          0   1

6. $\frac{1}{3}$ and $\frac{5}{8}$ ← + |———————————————| + →
                          0   1

7. $\frac{1}{6}$ and $\frac{3}{4}$ ← + |———————————————| + →
                          0   1

► Locate Fractions Greater Than 1

Locate each fraction on the number line.

8. $\frac{5}{4}$

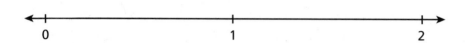

9. $\frac{8}{3}$

10. $\frac{5}{1}$

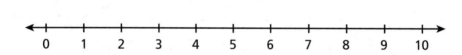

11. $\frac{8}{6}$

12. $\frac{6}{2}$

13. Explain how you located the fraction for one of the Exercises from 8–12.

_____

_____

_____

▶ Find 1

Locate 1 on each number line.

14.

15.

16.
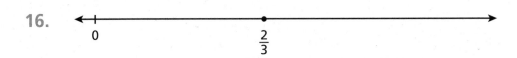

17.

18.

19. Explain how you located 1 for Exercise 17.

_____

_____

_____

▶ Find Fractions

Locate each fraction on the number line.
Draw another number line if you need to.

20. $\frac{3}{4}$

21. $\frac{5}{6}$

22. $\frac{2}{3}$

23. $\frac{7}{4}$

24. $\frac{7}{8}$

25. $\frac{10}{8}$

© Houghton Mifflin Harcourt Publishing Company

Name

Date

CA CC Content Standards **3.NF.3, 3.NF.3c, 3.NF.3d**
Mathematical Practices **MP.2**

► Compare Unit Fractions with Fraction Bars

The fraction bars are made up of unit fractions.
Look for patterns.

| $\frac{1}{1}$ | $\frac{1}{1}$ |

| $\frac{1}{2}$ | $\frac{1}{2}$ | $\frac{2}{2}$ |

| $\frac{1}{3}$ | $\frac{1}{3}$ | $\frac{1}{3}$ | $\frac{3}{3}$ |

| $\frac{1}{4}$ | $\frac{1}{4}$ | $\frac{1}{4}$ | $\frac{1}{4}$ | $\frac{4}{4}$ |

| $\frac{1}{5}$ | $\frac{1}{5}$ | $\frac{1}{5}$ | $\frac{1}{5}$ | $\frac{1}{5}$ | $\frac{5}{5}$ |

| $\frac{1}{6}$ | $\frac{1}{6}$ | $\frac{1}{6}$ | $\frac{1}{6}$ | $\frac{1}{6}$ | $\frac{1}{6}$ | $\frac{6}{6}$ |

| $\frac{1}{7}$ | $\frac{1}{7}$ | $\frac{1}{7}$ | $\frac{1}{7}$ | $\frac{1}{7}$ | $\frac{1}{7}$ | $\frac{1}{7}$ | $\frac{7}{7}$ |

| $\frac{1}{8}$ | $\frac{1}{8}$ | $\frac{1}{8}$ | $\frac{1}{8}$ | $\frac{1}{8}$ | $\frac{1}{8}$ | $\frac{1}{8}$ | $\frac{1}{8}$ | $\frac{8}{8}$ |

1. Describe two patterns that you see in the fraction bars.

_____

_____

_____

Compare.

2. $\frac{1}{3}$ $\bigcirc$ $\frac{1}{7}$

3. $\frac{1}{3}$ $\bigcirc$ $\frac{1}{2}$

4. $\frac{1}{6}$ $\bigcirc$ $\frac{1}{7}$

▶ Compare Unit Fractions with Number Lines

The number line shows unit fractions.
Look for patterns in the number line.

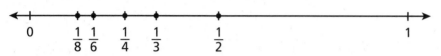

5. Describe a pattern that you see in the number line.

_____

_____

Compare. Use the fraction bars or the number line, if needed.

6. $\frac{1}{3}$ ◯ $\frac{1}{8}$ 7. $\frac{1}{4}$ ◯ $\frac{1}{2}$ 8. $\frac{1}{5}$ ◯ $\frac{1}{8}$

9. $\frac{1}{2}$ ◯ $\frac{1}{8}$ 10. $\frac{1}{4}$ ◯ $\frac{1}{7}$ 11. $\frac{1}{6}$ ◯ $\frac{1}{8}$

Solve. Use the fraction bars or the number line.

12. Between which two unit fractions would $\frac{1}{5}$ be on
the number line?

_____

13. Think about making a fraction bar for tenths.

   a. How many unit fractions would be in the fraction bar?

_____

   b. How do you write the unit fraction?

_____

14. **Predict** Can the fraction bars for any unit fractions
with even denominators always be split into
two equal parts? Explain your thinking.

_____

_____

Compare Unit Fractions

► Fraction Circles

Label each unit fraction.
Then cut out the fraction
circles on the dashed lines.

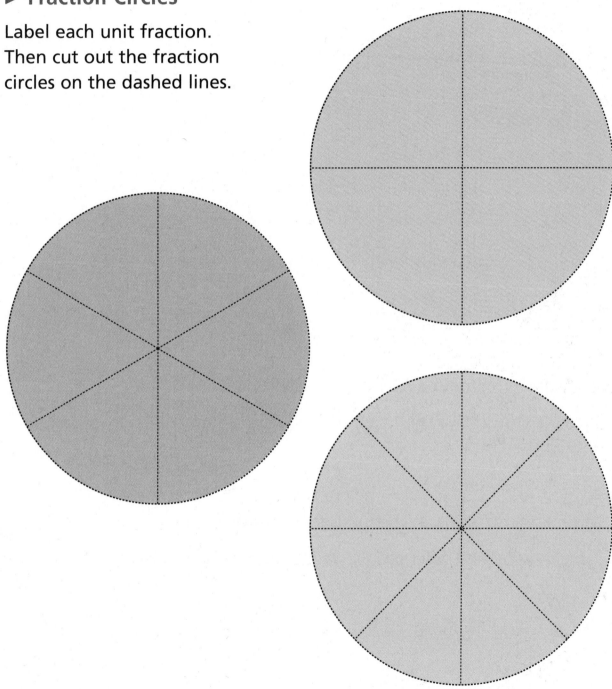

Compare Fractions **381A**

Name _____   **Date** _____

CA CC Content Standards **3.NF.1, 3.NF3d, 3.G.2**
Mathematical Practices **MP.2, MP.3, MP.6, MP.8**

▶ **Compare Fractions**

Use these two circles as wholes.

Work with a partner. Use your fraction circles to compare fractions during the class activity.

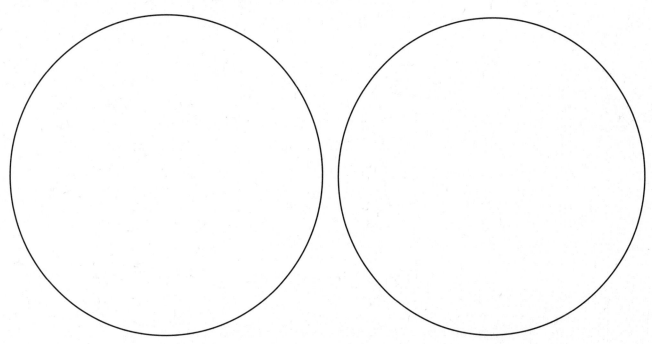

Record your work during the class activity.

1. $\frac{7}{8}$ ◯ $\frac{5}{8}$ 2. $\frac{3}{6}$ ◯ $\frac{5}{6}$

3. Explain how to compare two fractions that have the same denominator.

_____

_____

4. $\frac{3}{4}$ ◯ $\frac{3}{8}$ 5. $\frac{5}{8}$ ◯ $\frac{5}{6}$

6. Explain how to compare two fractions that have the same numerator.

_____

_____

► **Use Symbols to Compare Fractions**

Compare. Use <, >, or =.

7. $\frac{2}{2} \bigcirc \frac{2}{3}$

8. $\frac{1}{3} \bigcirc \frac{5}{3}$

9. $\frac{3}{2} \bigcirc \frac{3}{6}$

10. $\frac{5}{6} \bigcirc \frac{4}{6}$

11. $\frac{4}{6} \bigcirc \frac{5}{6}$

12. $\frac{3}{4} \bigcirc \frac{3}{8}$

13. $\frac{6}{3} \bigcirc \frac{5}{3}$

14. $\frac{8}{4} \bigcirc \frac{8}{7}$

15. $\frac{5}{6} \bigcirc \frac{5}{3}$

16. $\frac{8}{5} \bigcirc \frac{12}{5}$

17. $\frac{6}{5} \bigcirc \frac{6}{4}$

18. $\frac{2}{2} \bigcirc \frac{4}{4}$

19. $\frac{5}{8} \bigcirc \frac{3}{8}$

20. $\frac{7}{3} \bigcirc \frac{7}{6}$

21. $\frac{7}{8} \bigcirc \frac{3}{8}$

22. $\frac{9}{4} \bigcirc \frac{9}{8}$

23. $\frac{4}{4} \bigcirc \frac{6}{6}$

24. $\frac{12}{7} \bigcirc \frac{11}{7}$

25. $\frac{8}{6} \bigcirc \frac{8}{2}$

26. $\frac{8}{1} \bigcirc \frac{12}{1}$

► **What's the Error?**

Dear Math Students,

Today my teacher asked me to compare $\frac{3}{7}$ and $\frac{3}{9}$ and to explain my thinking.

I wrote $\frac{3}{7} = \frac{3}{9}$. My thinking is that both fractions have 3 unit fractions so they must be equal.

Is my work correct? If not, please correct my work and tell me what I did wrong. How do you know my answer is wrong?

Your friend,
Puzzled Penguin

27. Write an answer to Puzzled Penguin.

_____

_____

_____

_____

▶ Make Fraction Strips

▶ Halves, Fourths, and Eighths

Two fractions are **equivalent fractions** if they name the same part of a whole.

Use your halves, fourths, and eighths strips to complete Exercises 1–4.

$\frac{1}{2}$				$\frac{1}{2}$			
$\frac{1}{4}$		$\frac{1}{4}$		$\frac{1}{4}$		$\frac{1}{4}$	
$\frac{1}{8}$	$\frac{1}{8}$	$\frac{1}{8}$	$\frac{1}{8}$	$\frac{1}{8}$	$\frac{1}{8}$	$\frac{1}{8}$	$\frac{1}{8}$

1. If you compare your halves strip and your fourths strip, you can see that 2 fourths are the same as 1 half.

   Complete these two equations:

   _____ fourths = 1 half

   $$\frac{\square}{4} = \frac{1}{2}$$

2. How many eighths are in one half? _____

   Complete these two equations:

   _____ eighths = 1 half

   $$\frac{\square}{8} = \frac{1}{2}$$

3. What are two fractions that are equivalent to $\frac{1}{2}$?

   _____

4. How many eighths are in one fourth? _____

   Complete these two equations:

   _____ eighths = 1 fourth

   $$\frac{\square}{8} = \frac{1}{4}$$

© Houghton Mifflin Harcourt Publishing Company

► **Thirds and Sixths**

Use your thirds and sixths strips to answer Exercises 5–6.

5. How many sixths are in one third? _____

   Complete these two equations:

   _____ sixths = 1 third

   $$\frac{\boxed{}}{6} = \frac{1}{3}$$

6. How many sixths are in two thirds? _____

   Complete these two equations:

   _____ sixths = 2 thirds

   $$\frac{\boxed{}}{6} = \frac{2}{3}$$

► **What's the Error?**

Dear Math Students,

Today my teacher asked me to name a fraction that is equivalent to $\frac{1}{2}$.

I wrote $\frac{2}{6} = \frac{1}{2}$

Is my answer correct? If not, please correct my work and tell me what I did wrong.

Your Friend,
Puzzled Penguin

7. Write an answer to Puzzled Penguin.

   _____

   _____

   _____

Name _____ **Date** _____

CA CC Content Standards 3.NF.2a, 3.NF.2b, 3.NF.3, 3.NF.3a, 3.NF.3b, 3.NF.3c Mathematical Practices MP.1, MP.2

VOCABULARY
equivalence chain

▶ Equivalent Fractions on Number Lines

1. Complete each number line. Show all fractions including each fraction for 1.

halves

thirds $\frac{1}{3}$

fourths $\frac{1}{4}$

sixths $\frac{1}{6}$

eighths $\frac{1}{8}$

2. Write an **equivalence chain** with fractions that equal $\frac{2}{2}$.

_____

3. Why are the fractions in the equivalence chain for $\frac{2}{2}$ equal?

_____

4. Why does the length of unit fractions grow smaller as their denominators get larger?

_____

► Equivalence Chains

Use your number lines from page 385 to write an equivalence chain.

5. With fractions that equal $\frac{1}{2}$

    _____

6. With fractions that equal $\frac{1}{3}$

    _____

7. With fractions that equal $\frac{2}{3}$

    _____

8. With fractions that equal $\frac{1}{4}$

    _____

9. With fractions that equal $\frac{3}{4}$

    _____

10. With fractions that equal $\frac{8}{8}$

    _____

Solve. Use what you have learned about equivalent fractions and about comparing fractions.

Show your work.

11. Jaime has $\frac{1}{2}$ dozen red marbles and $\frac{4}{8}$ dozen green marbles. Does he have more red or green marbles?

    _____

12. Nancy buys $\frac{3}{6}$ pound of walnuts. Sandra buys $\frac{3}{4}$ pound of almonds. Who buys more nuts?

    _____

13. Chin and Maya collected shells at the beach. They both used the same kind of basket. Chin collected $\frac{3}{4}$ basket and Maya collected $\frac{3}{3}$ basket. Who collected more shells?

    _____

© Houghton Mifflin Harcourt Publishing Company

Equivalent Fractions

CA CC Content Standards 3.NF.3, 3.NF.3a, 3.NF.3b, 3.NF.3c, 3.NF.3d
Mathematical Practices MP.1, MP.2, MP.4

▶ Solve Fraction Problems

Solve. Draw diagrams or number lines if you need to.   *Show your work.*

1. The shelves in Roger's bookcase are $\frac{7}{8}$ yard long. Latanya's bookcase has shelves that are $\frac{5}{8}$ yard long. Whose bookcase has longer shelves? How do you know?

   _____

2. Rosa buys $\frac{3}{4}$ pound of cheddar cheese. Lucy buys $\frac{3}{8}$ pound of goat cheese. Who buys more cheese? Explain your answer.

   _____

3. Martha baked $\frac{8}{4}$ dozen cranberry muffins. Vera baked $\frac{8}{6}$ dozen banana muffins. Who baked fewer muffins? How do you know?

   _____

4. Lester walks $\frac{3}{4}$ mile to school. Bert said that he walks farther because he walks $\frac{6}{8}$ mile to school. Is his statement correct? Explain your answer.

   _____

5. Jack's family has a pickup truck that weighs $\frac{9}{4}$ ton. Ruth's family has a car that weighs $\frac{9}{8}$ ton. Is the pickup truck or the car heavier? How do you know?

   _____

6. Rusty painted $\frac{5}{6}$ of a mural for the school hallway. Has he painted more than half of the mural? Explain your answer.
   Hint: Find an equivalent fraction in sixths for $\frac{1}{2}$.

   _____

► Solve Fraction Problems (continued)

Solve. Draw diagrams or number lines if it helps.   *Show your work.*

7. Pearl used $\frac{3}{3}$ yard of fabric to make a pillow.
   Julia made her pillow from $\frac{4}{4}$ yard of fabric.
   They both paid $5 a yard for their fabric.
   Who paid more for fabric? How do you know?

   _____

   _____

8. At Binata's Bakery, two different recipes are
   used for wheat bread. For a round loaf, $\frac{5}{2}$ cups of
   wheat flour is used. For a long loaf, $\frac{7}{2}$ cups of
   wheat flour is used. For which kind of bread is
   more wheat flour used? Explain your answer.

   _____

   _____

9. Deena's water bottle can hold a total of $\frac{2}{5}$ liter
   of water. John's water bottle can hold a total of
   $\frac{5}{2}$ liter of water. Whose water bottle holds
   more water? How do you know?

   _____

   _____

10. Andy, Lu, and Carlos have $\frac{3}{3}$, $\frac{3}{4}$, and $\frac{3}{6}$ dozen
    pencils, but not in that order. Andy has the fewest
    pencils and Lu has the most. How many pencils
    does each boy have? Explain.

    _____

    _____

CA CC Content Standards **3.NF.1, 3.NF.3, 3.NF.3a, 3.NF.3b, 3.G.2**
Mathematical Practices **MP.2, MP.7**

▶ Math and Paper Folding

The art of paper folding began in China.
Later, Japan's version of paper folding,
called origami, became very popular.
Origami sculptures are made from a flat
sheet of square paper through folding and
sculpting techniques without cuts or glue.

Complete.

1. Fold a square sheet of paper in half diagonally.
   What part of the square is each triangle?

   _____

2. Fold the paper in half again. What part
   of the square is each triangle?

   _____

3. Fold the paper in half again. Open the paper.
   What part of the square is each triangle?

   _____

4. Explain how you know the eight parts
   have the same area.

   _____

   _____

5. Fold four triangles to the center as shown
   on the right. What part of the square is each
   triangle? Explain how you know.

   _____

   _____

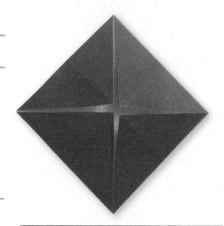

This basic origami fold is used
for making many objects.

► Math and Design

Complete.

6. Fold a square sheet of paper in half three times.
   Open the paper. Choose two different colors.
   Color every other rectangle or triangle one color.
   Color the other rectangles or triangles the second color.

7. Write 3 equivalent fractions for the part of the square
   that is colored the same color.

   _____

8. Predict the number of shapes you would make
   if you folded the square 4 times. Explain.

   _____

   _____

   _____

   _____

1. Select the way that shows the shaded fraction.
   Mark all that apply.

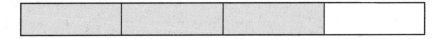

Ⓐ $\frac{1}{4}$

Ⓑ $\frac{4}{3}$

Ⓒ $\frac{3}{4}$

Ⓓ $\frac{1}{4} + \frac{1}{4} + \frac{1}{4}$

Ⓔ $\frac{4}{1} + \frac{4}{1} + \frac{4}{1}$

2. What unit fraction of the whole shape is the yellow triangle?
   Draw a line from the shape to the unit fraction the yellow triangle represents.

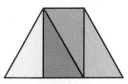

•   • $\frac{1}{8}$

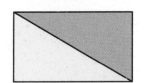

•   • $\frac{1}{6}$

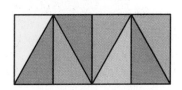

•   • $\frac{1}{4}$

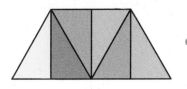

•   • $\frac{1}{2}$

3. Use a straightedge to divide the fraction bar
   into 6 equal parts. Then shade four parts.

   ├────────────── 1 whole ──────────────┤

   What fraction does the shaded fraction bar represent?

   _____

   Show the fraction as the sum of unit fractions.

   _____

4. Mark the number line to show the fractions. First
   divide the number line into correct unit fractions.

   $\frac{1}{8}$ $\frac{5}{8}$ $\frac{8}{8}$ $\frac{3}{4}$

   0   1

5. Write each fraction in the box to show whether it
   less than 1, equal to 1, or greater than 1.

   $\frac{6}{1}$ $\frac{1}{3}$ $\frac{4}{4}$ $\frac{3}{2}$ $\frac{5}{6}$

Less Than 1	Equal to 1	Greater Than 1

6. Use the fractions to label each point on the number line.

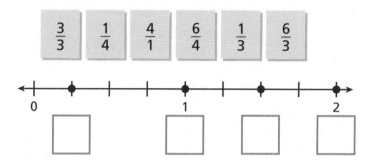

7. Select the fraction that would be included in an equivalence chain for $\frac{6}{6}$. Mark all that apply.

Ⓐ $\frac{3}{3}$

Ⓑ $\frac{3}{6}$

Ⓒ $\frac{4}{4}$

Ⓓ $\frac{5}{5}$

Ⓔ $\frac{6}{1}$

8. Choose the symbol that completes the comparison.

$\frac{10}{3}$ $\boxed{\begin{array}{c} < \\ > \\ = \end{array}}$ $\frac{10}{2}$

How did you know which symbol to choose?

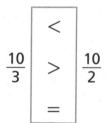

© Houghton Mifflin Harcourt Publishing Company

Name _____ Date _____

9. Noah compares $\frac{1}{3}$ to other fractions.

For numbers 9a–9d, select True or False for each statement.

9a. $\frac{1}{3} = \frac{2}{6}$ ○ True   ○ False

9b. $\frac{1}{3} > \frac{1}{4}$ ○ True   ○ False

9c. $\frac{1}{3} < \frac{3}{3}$ ○ True   ○ False

9d. $\frac{1}{3} = \frac{3}{1}$ ○ True   ○ False

10. Draw a line from the fraction on the left to match the equivalent fraction or number on the right.

$\frac{4}{6}$ •   • 8

$\frac{8}{1}$ •   • $\frac{2}{3}$

$\frac{3}{4}$ •   • 1

$\frac{2}{8}$ •   • $\frac{6}{8}$

$\frac{2}{2}$ •   • $\frac{1}{4}$

11. Diane's water bottle holds $\frac{5}{4}$ liter of water. Joe's holds $\frac{3}{4}$ liter of water. Write a comparison. Which water bottle holds more water?

Comparison: _____

_____ liter

12. Tyler picks $\frac{3}{3}$ dozen apples. Olivia picks $\frac{5}{6}$ dozen apples. Samantha picks $\frac{2}{3}$ dozen apples. Who picks the least number of apples?

_____

What strategy did you use to solve the problem?

13. Choose the fraction that makes the statement true.

$\frac{1}{3}$ would be between $\boxed{\begin{array}{c} \frac{1}{2} \\ \frac{2}{3} \\ \frac{1}{5} \end{array}}$ and $\frac{1}{4}$ on a number line.

14. Alyssa wants to write a fraction that is greater than $\frac{1}{6}$.

For numbers 14a–14d, choose Yes or No to tell whether Alyssa can write the fraction.

14a. $\frac{2}{1}$ ○ Yes   ○ No

14b. $\frac{1}{8}$ ○ Yes   ○ No

14c. $\frac{1}{5}$ ○ Yes   ○ No

14d. $\frac{8}{2}$ ○ Yes   ○ No

15. Dan walks $\frac{3}{8}$ mile to school. Beth walks $\frac{3}{4}$ mile to school.

Part A

Who walks farther? Label and shade the circles to help solve the problem.

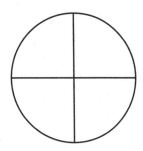 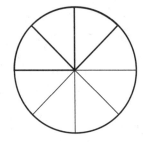

_____ walks farther.

Part B

Suppose Dan walks $\frac{6}{8}$ mile instead of $\frac{3}{8}$ mile. Who walks farther? How do the circles help you decide?

16. Henry and Reiko both use 1 yard of ribbon to make bows. Write two different fractions to show that Henry and Reiko use the same amount of ribbon.

Henry uses _____ yard.

Reiko uses _____ yard.

Reference Tables

Table of Measures	
Metric	**Customary**
Length/Area	

1 meter (m) = 10 decimeters (dm)
1 meter (m) = 100 centimeters (cm)
1 decimeter (dm) = 10 centimeters (cm)
1 square centimeter = 1 cm²
   A metric unit for measuring area. It is the area of a square that is one centimeter on each side.
	1 foot (ft) = 12 inches (in.)
	1 yard = 3 feet (ft)
	1 mile (mi) = 5,280 feet (ft)
	1 square inch = 1 in²
	   A customary unit for measuring area. It is the area of a square that is one inch on each side.

Liquid Volume	
1 liter (L) = 1,000 milliliters (mL)	1 tablespoon (tbsp) = $\frac{1}{2}$ fluid ounce (fl oz) 1 cup (c) = 8 fluid ounces (fl oz) 1 pint (pt) = 2 cups (c) 1 quart (qt) = 2 pints (pt) 1 gallon (gal) = 4 quarts (qt)

Reference Tables (continued)

Table of Units of Time

Time

1 minute (min) = 60 seconds (sec)

1 hour (hr) = 60 minutes

1 day = 24 hours

1 week (wk) = 7 days

1 month, about 30 days

1 year (yr) = 12 months (mo)
or about 52 weeks

1 year = 365 days

1 leap year = 366 days

Properties of Operations

Associative Property of Addition

$(a + b) + c = a + (b + c)$ $(2 + 5) + 3 = 2 + (5 + 3)$

Commutative Property of Addition

$a + b = b + a$ $4 + 6 = 6 + 4$

Identity Property of Addition

$a + 0 = 0 + a = a$ $3 + 0 = 0 + 3 = 3$

Associative Property of Multiplication

$(a \cdot b) \cdot c = a \cdot (b \cdot c)$ $(3 \cdot 5) \cdot 7 = 3 \cdot (5 \cdot 7)$

Commutative Property of Multiplication

$a \cdot b = b \cdot a$ $6 \cdot 3 = 3 \cdot 6$

Identity Property of Multiplication

$a \cdot 1 = 1 \cdot a = a$ $8 \cdot 1 = 1 \cdot 8 = 8$

Zero Property of Multiplication

$a \cdot 0 = 0 \cdot a = 0$ $5 \cdot 0 = 0 \cdot 5 = 0$

Distributive Property of Multiplication over Addition

$a \cdot (b + c) = (a \cdot b) + (a \cdot c)$ $2 \cdot (4 + 3) = (2 \cdot 4) + (2 \cdot 3)$

Problem Types

Addition and Subtraction Problem Types

	Result Unknown	Change Unknown	Start Unknown
Add to	Aisha had 274 stamps in her collection. Then her grandfather gave her 65 stamps. How many stamps does she have now? *Situation and solution equation:*[1] $274 + 65 = s$	Aisha had 274 stamps in her collection. Then her grandfather gave her some stamps. Now she has 339 stamps. How many stamps did her grandfather give her? *Situation equation:* $274 + s = 339$ *Solution equation:* $s = 339 - 274$	Aisha had some stamps in her collection. Then her grandfather gave her 65 stamps. Now she has 339 stamps. How many stamps did she have to start? *Situation equation* $s + 65 = 339$ *Solution equation:* $s = 339 - 65$
Take from	A store had 750 bottles of water at the start of the day. During the day, the store sold 490 bottles. How many bottles did they have at the end of the day? *Situation and solution equation:* $750 - 490 = b$	A store had 750 bottles of water at the start of the day. The store had 260 bottles left at the end of the day. How many bottles did the store sell? *Situation equation:* $750 - b = 260$ *Solution equation:* $b = 750 - 260$	A store had a number of bottles of water at the start of the day. The store sold 490 bottles of water. At the end of the day 260 bottles were left. How many bottles did the store have to start with? *Situation equation:* $b - 490 = 260$ *Solution equation:* $b = 260 + 490$

[1]A situation equation represents the structure (action) in the problem situation. A solution equation shows the operation used to find the answer.

	Total Unknown	Addend Unknown	Both Addends Unknown
Put Together/ Take Apart	A clothing store has 375 shirts with short sleeves and 148 shirts with long sleeves. How many shirts does the store have in all? *Math drawing:* s 375 148 *Situation and solution equation:* $375 + 148 = s$	Of the 523 shirts in a clothing store, 375 have short sleeves. The rest have long sleeves. How many shirts have long sleeves? *Math drawing:* 523 375 l *Situation equation:* $523 = 375 + l$ *Solution equation:* $l = 523 - 375$	A clothing store has 523 shirts. Some have short sleeves and some have long sleeves. How many of the shirts have short sleeves and how many have long sleeves? *Math drawing:* 523 s l *Situation equation* $523 = s + l$

Problem Types continued

Addition and Subtraction Problem Types (continued)

	Difference Unknown	Greater Unknown	Smaller Unknown
Compare	At a zoo, the female black bear weighs 175 pounds. The male black bear weighs 260 pounds. How much more does the male black bear weigh than the female black bear? At a zoo, the female black bear weighs 175 pounds. The male black bear weighs 260 pounds. How much less does the female black bear weigh than the male black bear? *Math drawing:* 260 175 | d *Situation equation:* $175 + d = 260$ or $d = 260 - 175$ *Solution equation:* $d = 260 - 175$	**Leading Language** At a zoo, the female black bear weighs 175 pounds. The male black bear weighs 85 pounds more than the female black bear. How much does the male black bear weigh? **Misleading Language** At a zoo, the female black bear weighs 175 pounds. The female black bear weighs 85 pounds less than the male black bear. How much does the male black bear weigh? *Math drawing:* m 175 | 85 *Situation and solution equation:* $175 + 85 = m$	**Leading Language** At a zoo, the male black bear weighs 260 pounds. The female black bear weighs 85 pounds less than the male black bear. How much does the female black bear weigh? **Misleading Language** At a zoo, the male black bear weighs 260 pounds. The male black bear weighs 85 pounds more than the female black bear. How much does the female black bear weigh? *Math drawing:* 260 f | 85 *Situation equation* $f + 85 = 260$ or $f = 260 - 85$ *Solution equation:* $f = 260 - 85$

A comparison sentence can always be said in two ways. One way uses *more*, and the other uses *fewer* or *less*. Misleading language suggests the wrong operation. For example, it says *the female black bear weighs 85 pounds less than the male*, but you have to add 85 pounds to the female's weight to get the male's weight.

Multiplication and Division Problem Types

	Unknown Product	Group Size Unknown	Number of Groups Unknown
Equal Groups	A teacher bought 5 boxes of markers. There are 8 markers in each box. How many markers did the teacher buy? *Math drawing:* *Situation and solution equation:* $n = 5 \cdot 8$	A teacher bought 5 boxes of markers. She bought 40 markers in all. How many markers are in each box? *Math drawing:* *Situation equation:* $5 \cdot n = 40$ *Solution equation:* $n = 40 \div 5$	A teacher bought boxes of 8 markers. She bought 40 markers in all. How many boxes of markers did she buy? *Math drawing:* *Situation equation* $n \cdot 8 = 40$ *Solution equation:* $n = 40 \div 8$

Problem Types (continued)

	Unknown Product	Unknown Factor	Unknown Factor
Arrays	For the yearbook photo, the drama club stood in 3 rows of 7 students. How many students were in the photo in all? *Math drawing:* 7 ○○○○○○○ 3 ○○○○○○○ ○○○○○○○ *Situation and solution equation:* $n = 3 \cdot 7$	For the yearbook photo, the 21 students in drama club, stood in 3 equal rows. How many students were in each row? *Math drawing:* n n ⟩ Total: 21 n *Situation equation:* $3 \cdot n = 21$ *Solution equation:* $n = 21 \div 3$	For the yearbook photo, the 21 students in drama club, stood in rows of 7 students. How many rows were there? *Math drawing:* 7 7 ⟩ Total: 21 7 *Situation equation* $n \cdot 7 = 21$ *Solution equation:* $n = 21 \div 7$
Area	The floor of the kitchen is 2 meters by 5 meters. What is the area of the floor? *Math drawing:* 5 2 [A] *Situation and solution equation:* $A = 5 \cdot 2$	The floor of the kitchen is 5 meters long. The area of the floor is 10 square meters. What is the width of the floor? *Math drawing:* 5 w [10] *Situation equation:* $5 \cdot w = 10$ *Solution equation:* $w = 10 \div 5$	The floor of the kitchen is 2 meters wide. The area of the floor is 10 square meters. What is the length of the floor? *Math drawing:* l 2 [10] *Situation equation* $l \cdot 2 = 10$ *Solution equation:* $l = 10 \div 2$

© Houghton Mifflin Harcourt Publishing Company

Vocabulary Activities

▶ Word Review [PAIRS]

Work with a partner. Choose a word from a current unit or a review word from a previous unit. Use the word to complete one of the activities listed on the right. Then ask your partner if they have any edits to your work or questions about what you described. Repeat, having your partner choose a word.

Activities

- ▶ Give the meaning in words or gestures.
- ▶ Use the word in the sentence.
- ▶ Give another word that is related to the word in some way and explain the relationship.

▶ Crossword Puzzle [PAIRS] OR [INDIVIDUALS]

Create a crossword puzzle similar to the example below. Use vocabulary words from the unit. You can add other related words, too. Challenge your partner to solve the puzzle.

Across

1. _____ and subtraction are inverse operations.

2. To put amounts together

3. When you trade 10 ones for 1 ten, you _____.

4. The answer to an addition problem

Down

1. In 24 + 65 = 89, 24 is an _____.

3. A combination of the digits 0, 1, 2, 3, 4, 5, 6, 7, 8, and 9.

4. The operation that you can use to find out how much more one number is than another.

Vocabulary Activities (continued)

▶ Word Wall PAIRS OR SMALL GROUPS

With your teacher's permission, start a word wall in your classroom. As you work through each lesson, put the math vocabulary words on index cards and place them on the word wall. You can work with a partner or a small group choosing a word and giving the definition.

▶ Word Web INDIVIDUALS

Make a word web for a word or words you do not understand in a unit. Fill in the web with words or phrases that are related to the vocabulary word.

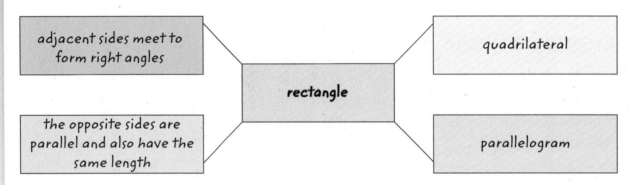

adjacent sides meet to form right angles

the opposite sides are parallel and also have the same length

rectangle

quadrilateral

parallelogram

▶ Alphabet Challenge PAIRS OR INDIVIDUALS

Take an alphabet challenge. Choose 3 letters from the alphabet. Think of three vocabulary words for each letter. Then write the definition or draw an example for each word.

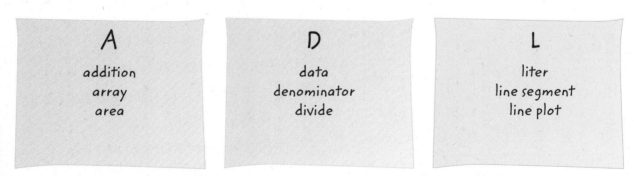

A
addition
array
area

D
data
denominator
divide

L
liter
line segment
line plot

▶ Concentration PAIRS

Write the vocabulary words and related words from a unit on index cards. Write the definitions on a different set of index cards. Mix up both sets of cards. Then place the cards facedown on a table in an array, for example, 3 by 3 or 3 by 4. Take turns turning over two cards. If one card is a word and one card is a definition that matches the word, take the pair. Continue until each word has been matched with its definition.

area

the number of square units in a region

▶ Math Journal INDIVIDUALS

As you learn new words, write them in your Math Journal. Write the definition of the word and include a sketch or an example. As you learn new information about the word, add notes to your definition.

polygon: a closed plane figure with sides made of straight line segments.

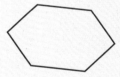

In concave polygons, there exists a line segment with endpoints inside the polygon and a point on the line segment that is outside the polygon.

▶ What's the Word? PAIRS

Work together to make a poster or bulletin board display of the words in a unit. Write definitions on a set of index cards. Mix up the cards. Work with a partner, choosing a definition from the index cards. Have your partner point to the word on the poster and name the matching math vocabulary word. Switch roles and try the activity again.

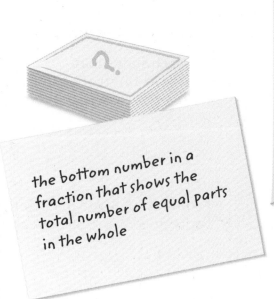

fraction   fourths

unit fraction   eighths

denominator   halves

numerator   sixths

equivalent

equivalent fractions

equivalence chain

thirds

the bottom number in a fraction that shows the total number of equal parts in the whole

Glossary

A

addend One of two or more numbers to be added together to find a sum.

Example: $8 + 4 = 12$

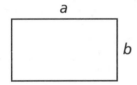
addend   addend   sum

addition A mathematical operation that combines two or more numbers.

Example: $23 + 52 = 75$

addend   addend   sum

adjacent (sides) Two sides of a figure that meet at a point.

Example: Sides a and b are adjacent.

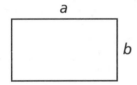

A.M. The time period between midnight and noon.

analog clock A clock with a face and hands.

angle A figure formed by two rays or two line segments that meet at an endpoint.

area The total number of square units that cover a figure.

Example: The area of the rectangle is 6 square units.

array An arrangement of objects, pictures, or numbers in columns and rows.

Associative Property of Addition (Grouping Property of Addition)

The property which states that changing the way in which addends are grouped does not change the sum.

Example: $(2 + 3) + 1 = 2 + (3 + 1)$

$5 + 1 = 2 + 4$

$6 = 6$

Associative Property of Multiplication (Grouping Property of Multiplication)

The property which states that changing the way in which factors are grouped does not change the product.

Example: $(2 \times 3) \times 4 = 2 \times (3 \times 4)$

$6 \times 4 = 2 \times 12$

$24 = 24$

Glossary (continued)

axis (plural: **axes**) A reference line for a graph. A graph has 2 axes; one is horizontal and the other is vertical.

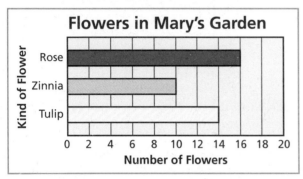

Flowers in Mary's Garden

B

---

bar graph A graph that uses bars to show data. The bars may be horizontal, as in the graph above, or vertical, as in the graph below.

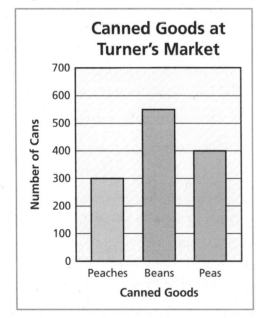

C

---

capacity The amount a container can hold.

centimeter (cm) A metric unit used to measure length.

100 centimeters = 1 meter

column A part of a table or array that contains items arranged vertically.

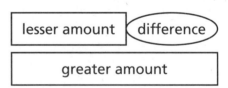

Commutative Property of Addition (Order Property of Addition) The property which states that changing the order of addends does not change the sum.

Example: 3 + 7 = 7 + 3

10 = 10

Commutative Property of Multiplication (Order Property of Multiplication) The property which states that changing the order of factors does not change the product.

Example: $5 \times 4 = 4 \times 5$

20 = 20

comparison bars Bars that represent the greater amount, lesser amount, and difference in a comparison problem.

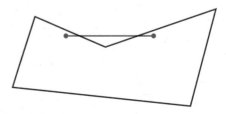

concave A polygon for which you can connect two points inside the polygon with a segment that passes outside the polygon.

convex A polygon is convex if all of its diagonals are inside it.

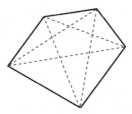

cup (c) A customary unit of measure used to measure capacity.

1 cup = 8 fluid ounces
2 cups = 1 pint
4 cups = 1 quart
16 cups = 1 gallon

D

data Pieces of information.

decagon A polygon with 10 sides.

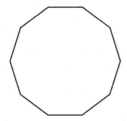

decimeter (dm) A metric unit used to measure length

1 decimeter = 10 centimeters

denominator The bottom number in a fraction that shows the total number of equal parts in the whole.

Example: $\frac{1}{3}$ ◄——— denominator

diagonal A line segment that connects two corners of a figure and is not a side of the figure.

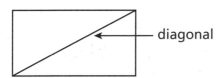
diagonal

difference The result of subtraction or of comparing.

digit Any of the symbols 0, 1, 2, 3, 4, 5, 6, 7, 8, 9.

digital clock A clock that displays the hour and minutes with numbers.

Distributive property You can multiply a sum by a number, or multiply each addend by the number and add the products; the result is the same.

Example:

$$3 \times (2 + 4) = (3 \times 2) + (3 \times 4)$$
$$3 \times 6 \quad = \quad 6 \quad + \quad 12$$
$$18 \quad = \quad 18$$

dividend The number that is divided in division.

Examples:

$$12 \div 3 = 4 \qquad 3\overline{)12}^{\,4}$$

dividend   dividend

division The mathematical operation that separates an amount into smaller equal groups to find the number of groups or the number in each group.

Example: $12 \div 3 = 4$ is a division number sentence.

divisor The number that you divide by in division.

Example: $12 \div 3 = 4 \qquad 3\overline{)12}^{\,4}$

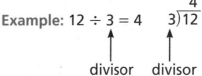
divisor   divisor

Glossary (continued)

E

elapsed time The time that passes between the beginning and the end of an activity.

endpoint The point at either end of a line segment or the beginning point of a ray.

endpoint   endpoint   endpoint

equation A mathematical sentence with an equals sign.

Examples: 11 + 22 = 33
75 − 25 = 50

equivalent Equal, or naming the same amount.

equivalent fractions Fractions that name the same amount.

Example: $\frac{1}{2}$ and $\frac{2}{4}$

equivalent fractions

estimate About how many or about how much.

even number A whole number that is a multiple of 2. The ones digit in an even number is 0, 2, 4, 6, or 8.

expanded form A number written to show the value of each of its digits.

Examples:
347 = 300 + 40 + 7
347 = 3 hundreds + 4 tens + 7 ones

expression A combination of numbers, variables, and/or operation signs. An expression does not have an equals sign.

Examples: 4 + 7 $a − 3$

F

factors Numbers that are multiplied to give a product.

Example: 4 × 5 = 20

factor   factor   product

fluid ounce (fl oz) A unit of liquid volume in the customary system that equals $\frac{1}{8}$ cup or 2 tablespoons.

foot (ft) A customary unit used to measure length.

1 foot = 12 inches

fraction A number that names part of a whole or part of a set.

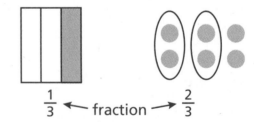

$\frac{1}{3}$ ← fraction → $\frac{2}{3}$

frequency table A table that shows how many times each event, item, or category occurs.

Frequency Table	
Age	Tally
7	1
8	3
9	5
10	4
11	2

function table A table of ordered pairs that shows a function.

For every input number, there is only one possible output number.

Rule: add 2	
Input	Output
1	3
2	4
3	5
4	6

G

gallon (gal) A customary unit used to measure capacity.

1 gallon = 4 quarts = 8 pints = 16 cups

gram (g) A metric unit of mass. One paper clip has a mass of about 1 gram.

1,000 grams = 1 kilogram

greater than (>) A symbol used to compare two numbers.

Example: 6 > 5
  6 *is greater than* 5.

group To combine numbers to form new tens, hundreds, thousands, and so on.

H

height A vertical distance, or how tall something is.

hexagon A polygon with six sides.

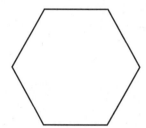

horizontal Extending in two directions, left and right.

horizontal bar graph A bar graph with horizontal bars.

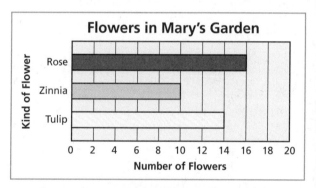

I

Identity Property of Addition If 0 is added to a number, the sum equals that number.

Example: 3 + 0 = 3

Identity Property of Multiplication The product of 1 and any number equals that number.

Example: 10 × 1 = 10

Glossary (continued)

improper fraction A fraction in which the numerator is equal to or is greater than the denominator. Improper fractions are equal to or greater than 1. $\frac{5}{5}$ and $\frac{8}{3}$ are improper fractions.

inch (in.) A customary unit used to measure length.

12 inches = 1 foot

K

key A part of a map, graph, or chart that explains what symbols mean.

kilogram (kg) A metric unit of mass.

1 kilogram = 1,000 grams

kilometer (km) A metric unit of length.

1 kilometer = 1,000 meters

L

less than (<) A symbol used to compare numbers.

Example: 5 < 6

5 *is less than* 6.

line A straight path that goes on forever in opposite directions.

line plot A diagram that shows frequency of data on a number line. Also called a *dot plot*.

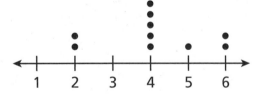

line segment A part of a line. A line segment has two endpoints.

liquid volume A measure of how much a container can hold. Also called *capacity*.

liter (L) A metric unit used to measure capacity.

1 liter = 1,000 milliliters

M

mass The amount of matter in an object.

mental math A way to solve problems without using pencil and paper or a calculator.

meter (m) A metric unit used to measure length.

1 meter = 100 centimeters

method A procedure, or way, of doing something.

mile (mi) A customary unit of length.

1 mile = 5,280 feet

milliliter (mL) A metric unit used to measure capacity.

1,000 milliliters = 1 liter

mixed number A whole number and a fraction.

$1\frac{3}{4}$ is a mixed number.

multiple A number that is the product of the given number and any whole number.

multiplication A mathematical operation that combines equal groups.

Example: $4 \times 3 = 12$

factor   factor   product

$3 + 3 + 3 + 3 = 12$

4 times

N

number line A line on which numbers are assigned to lengths.

numerator The top number in a fraction that shows the number of equal parts counted.

Example: $\frac{1}{3}$ ← numerator

O

octagon A polygon with eight sides.

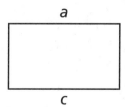

odd number A whole number that is not a multiple of 2. The ones digit in an odd number is 1, 3, 5, 7, or 9.

opposite sides Sides of a polygon that are across from each other; they do not meet at a point.

Example: Sides *a* and *c* are opposite.

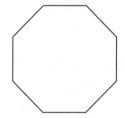

Order of operations A set of rules that state the order in which the operations in an expression should be done.

STEP 1: Perform operations inside parentheses first.

STEP 2: Multiply and divide from left to right.

STEP 3: Add and subtract from left to right.

ounce (oz) A customary unit used to measure weight.

16 ounces = 1 pound

P

parallel lines Two lines that are the same distance apart.

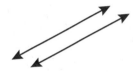

parallelogram A quadrilateral with both pairs of opposite sides parallel.

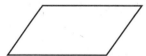

pentagon A polygon with five sides.

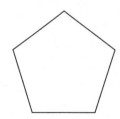

Glossary (continued)

perimeter The distance around a figure.

Example:

Perimeter = 3 cm + 5 cm + 3 cm + 5 cm = 16 cm

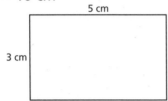

pictograph A graph that uses pictures or symbols to represent data.

Favorite Ice Cream Flavors

Peanut Butter Crunch	🍦 🍦
Cherry Vanilla	🍦 🍦 🍦
Chocolate	🍦 🍦 🍦 🍦

Each 🍦 stands for 4 votes.

pint (pt) A customary unit used to measure capacity.

1 pint = 2 cups

place value The value assigned to the place that a digit occupies in a number.

9   6   2
↑   ↑   ↑
hundreds tens ones

place value drawing A drawing that represents a number. Hundreds are represented by boxes, tens by vertical lines, and ones by small circles.

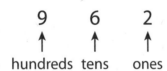

P.M. The time period between noon and midnight.

polygon A closed plane figure with sides made up of straight line segments.

pound (lb) A customary unit used to measure weight.

1 pound = 16 ounces

product The answer when you multiply numbers.

Example: 4 × 7 = 28

factor   factor   product

proof drawing A drawing used to show that an answer is correct.

249
+ 386
  11
635

Q

quadrilateral A polygon with four sides.

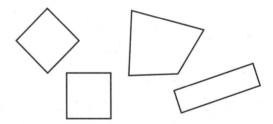

quart (qt) A customary unit used to measure capacity.

1 quart = 4 cups

quotient The answer when you divide numbers.

Examples: 5 ← quotient
35 ÷ 7 = 5   7)35
      ↑
   quotient

© Houghton Mifflin Harcourt Publishing Company

ray A part of a line that has one endpoint and goes on forever in one direction.

rectangle A parallelogram that has 4 right angles.

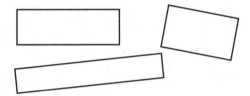

rhombus A parallelogram with equal sides.

right angle An angle that measures 90°.

round To find about how many or how much by expressing a number to the nearest ten, hundred, thousand, and so on.

row A part of a table or array that contains items arranged horizontally.

scale An arrangement of numbers in order with equal intervals.

side (of a figure) One of the line segments that make up a polygon.

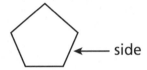

simplify To write an equivalent fraction with a smaller numerator and denominator.

situation equation An equation that shows the action or the relationship in a problem.

Example: $35 + n = 40$

solution equation An equation that shows the operation to perform in order to solve the problem.

Example: $n = 40 - 35$

square A rectangle with four sides of the same length.

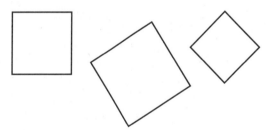

square number The product of a whole number and itself.

Example: $4 \times 4 = 16$

square number

Glossary (continued)

square unit A unit of area equal to the area of a square with one-unit sides.

standard form The name of a number written using digits.

Example: 1,829

subtract To find the difference of two numbers.

Example: $18 - 11 = 7$

subtraction A mathematical operation on two numbers that gives the difference.

Example: $43 - 40 = 3$

sum The answer when adding two or more addends.

Example: $37 + 52 = 89$

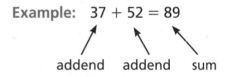

addend   addend   sum

T

table An easy-to-read arrangement of data, usually in rows and columns.

Favorite Team Sport	
Sport	Number of Students
Baseball	35
Soccer	60
Basketball	40

tally marks Short line segments drawn in groups of 5. Each mark, including the slanted mark, stands for 1 unit.

means 13
5 5 3

total The answer when adding two or more addends. The sum of two or more numbers.

Example: $672 + 228 = 900$

addend   addend   total   sum

trapezoid A quadrilateral with exactly one pair of parallel sides.

triangle A polygon with three sides.

U

ungroup To open up 1 in a given place to make 10 of the next smaller place value in order to subtract.

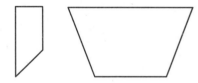

unit fraction A fraction whose numerator is 1. It shows one equal part of a whole.

Example: $\frac{1}{4}$

unit square A square whose area is 1 square unit.

V

variable A letter or symbol used to represent an unknown number in an algebraic expression or equation.

Example: $2 + n$

   n is a variable.

Venn diagram A diagram that uses circles to show the relationship among sets of objects.

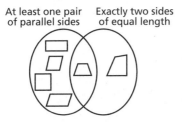

vertex A point where sides, rays, or edges meet.

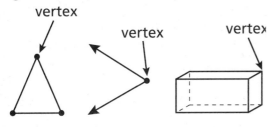

vertical Extending in two directions, up and down.

vertical bar graph A bar graph with vertical bars.

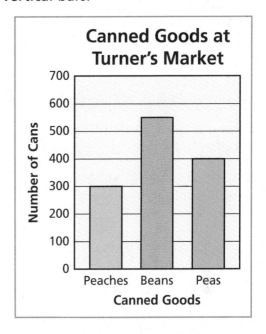

W

weight The measure of how heavy something is.

word form A name of a number written using words instead of digits.

Example: Nine hundred eighty-four

Glossary (continued)

Y

yard (yd) A customary unit used to measure length.

1 yard = 3 feet = 36 inches

Z

Zero Property of Multiplication If 0 is multiplied by a number, the product is 0.

Example: $3 \times 0 = 0$

California Common Core Standards for Mathematical Content

3.OA Operations and Algebraic Thinking

Represent and solve problems involving multiplication and division.

3.OA.1	Interpret products of whole numbers, e.g., interpret 5×7 as the total number of objects in 5 groups of 7 objects each.	Unit 1 Lessons 1, 2, 3, 4, 5, 6, 7, 8, 9, 10, 12, 13, 14, 16, 18, 19; Unit 2 Lessons 2, 4, 7, 9, 10, 11, 13, 15
3.OA.2	Interpret whole-number quotients of whole numbers, e.g., interpret $56 \div 8$ as the number of objects in each share when 56 objects are partitioned equally into 8 shares, or as a number of shares when 56 objects are partitioned into equal shares of 8 objects each.	Unit 1 Lessons 4, 5, 6, 7, 9, 10, 12, 13, 14, 15, 16, 17, 18, 19; Unit 2 Lessons 2, 4, 7, 9, 10, 11, 13, 15
3.OA.3	Use multiplication and division within 100 to solve word problems in situations involving equal groups, arrays, and measurement quantities, e.g., by using drawings and equations with a symbol for the unknown number to represent the problem.	Unit 1 Lessons 2, 3, 4, 5, 6, 7, 9, 10, 12, 13, 14, 16, 18, 19; Unit 2 Lessons 2, 4, 7, 9, 10, 11, 13, 15; Unit 3 Lessons 2, 3, 4, 5, 14; Unit 5 Lessons 2, 3, 7, 8, 9, 11
3.OA.4	Determine the unknown whole number in a multiplication or division equation relating three whole numbers.	Unit 1 Lessons 1, 4, 5, 6, 7, 8, 9, 10, 11, 12, 13, 14, 16, 18, 19; Unit 2 Lessons 1, 2, 3, 4, 5, 6, 7, 8, 9, 10, 11, 13, 14, 15; Unit 5 Lessons 2, 3

Understand properties of multiplication and the relationship between multiplication and division.

3.OA.5	Apply properties of operations as strategies to multiply and divide.	Unit 1 Lessons 3, 6, 11, 12, 14, 15, 19; Unit 2 Lessons 1, 8, 12, 15
3.OA.6	Understand division as an unknown-factor problem.	Unit 1 Lessons 4, 5, 6, 7, 8, 9, 10, 11, 12, 13, 14, 15, 16, 17, 18; Unit 2 Lessons 1, 2, 3, 4, 5, 6, 7, 8, 9, 10, 11, 12, 13, 14

Multiply and divide within 100.

3.OA.7	Fluently multiply and divide within 100, using strategies such as the relationship between multiplication and division or properties of operations. By the end of Grade 3, know from memory all products of two one-digit numbers.	Unit 1 Lessons 1, 2, 3, 4, 5, 6, 7, 8, 9, 10, 11, 12, 13, 14, 15, 16, 17, 18, 19; Unit 2 Lessons 1, 2, 3, 4, 5, 6, 7, 8, 9, 10, 11, 12, 13, 14, 15

Solve problems involving the four operations, and identify and explain patterns in arithmetic.

3.OA.8	Solve two-step word problems using the four operations. Represent these problems using equations with a letter standing for the unknown quantity. Assess the reasonableness of answers using mental computation and estimation strategies including rounding.	Unit 2 Lessons 9, 10, 11, 13; Unit 3 Lesson 17; Unit 4 Lesson 17; Unit 5 Lessons 7, 8, 9, 10, 11

3.OA.9	Identify arithmetic patterns (including patterns in the addition table or multiplication table), and explain them using properties of operations.	Unit 1 Lessons 1, 5, 6, 7, 8, 10, 12, 15, 19; Unit 2 Lessons 1, 3, 5, 6, 8, 14, 15; Unit 4 Lesson 17

3.NBT Number and Operations in Base Ten

Use place value understanding and properties of operations to perform multi-digit arithmetic.

3.NBT.1	Use place value understanding to round whole numbers to the nearest 10 or 100.	Unit 4 Lessons 1, 2, 3, 4, 5, 6, 10, 17, 18; Unit 5 Lesson 4
3.NBT.2	Fluently add and subtract within 1000 using strategies and algorithms based on place value, properties of operations, and/or the relationship between addition and subtraction.	Unit 3 Lessons 11, 12; Unit 4 Lessons 1, 2, 3, 4, 5, 6, 7, 8, 9, 10, 11, 12, 13, 14, 15, 16, 17, 18; Unit 5 Lessons 1, 2, 3, 4, 5, 6, 8, 9, 10, 11
3.NBT.3	Multiply one-digit whole numbers by multiples of 10 in the range 10–90 (e.g., 9×80, 5×60) using strategies based on place value and properties of operations.	Unit 2 Lesson 12

3.NF Number and Operations–Fractions

Develop understanding of fractions as numbers.

3.NF.1	Understand a fraction $\frac{1}{b}$ as the quantity formed by 1 part when a whole is partitioned into b equal parts; understand a fraction $\frac{a}{b}$ as the quantity formed by a parts of size $\frac{1}{b}$.	Unit 7 Lessons 1, 2, 9
3.NF.2	Understand a fraction as a number on the number line; represent fractions on a number line diagram.	Unit 7 Lesson 2, 3, 4, 8
3.NF.2a	Represent a fraction $\frac{1}{b}$ on a number line diagram by defining the interval from 0 to 1 as the whole and partitioning it into b equal parts. Recognize that each part has size $\frac{1}{b}$ and that the endpoint of the part based at 0 locates the number $\frac{1}{b}$ on the number line.	Unit 7 Lessons 2, 3, 4, 8
3.NF.2b	Represent a fraction $\frac{a}{b}$ on a number line diagram by marking off a lengths $\frac{1}{b}$ from 0. Recognize that the resulting interval has size $\frac{a}{b}$ and that its endpoint locates the number $\frac{1}{b}$ on the number line.	Unit 7 Lessons 2, 3, 4, 8
3.NF.3	Explain equivalence of fractions in special cases, and compare fractions by reasoning about their size.	Unit 7 Lessons 4, 5, 6, 7, 8, 9
3.NF.3a	Understand two fractions as equivalent (equal) if they are the same size, or the same point on a number line.	Unit 7 Lessons 6, 7, 8, 9
3.NF.3b	Recognize and generate simple equivalent fractions, e.g., $\frac{1}{2} = \frac{2}{4}, \frac{4}{6} = \frac{2}{3}$. Explain why the fractions are equivalent, e.g., by using a visual fraction model.	Unit 7 Lessons 6, 7, 8, 9
3.NF.3c	Express whole numbers as fractions, and recognize fractions that are equivalent to whole numbers.	Unit 7 Lesson 3, 4, 7, 8

3.NF.3d	Compare two fractions with the same numerator or the same denominator by reasoning about their size. Recognize that comparisons are valid only when the two fractions refer to the same whole. Record the results of comparisons with the symbols $>$, $=$, or $<$, and justify the conclusions, e.g., by using a visual fraction model.	Unit 7 Lessons 4, 5, 8, 9

3.MD Measurement and Data

Solve problems involving measurement and estimation of intervals of time, liquid volumes, and masses of objects.

3.MD.1	Tell and write time to the nearest minute and measure time intervals in minutes. Solve word problems involving addition and subtraction of time intervals in minutes, e.g., by representing the problem on a number line diagram.	Unit 3 Lessons 6, 7, 8, 9, 10, 15
3.MD.2	Measure and estimate liquid volumes and masses of objects using standard units of grams (g), kilograms (kg), and liters (l). Add, subtract, multiply, or divide to solve one-step word problems involving masses or volumes that are given in the same units, e.g., by using drawings (such as a beaker with a measurement scale) to represent the problem.	Unit 3 Lessons 2, 3, 4, 5

Represent and interpret data.

3.MD.3	Draw a scaled picture graph and a scaled bar graph to represent a data set with several categories. Solve one- and two-step "how many more" and "how many less" problems using information presented in scaled bar graphs.	Unit 3 Lessons 11, 12, 14
3.MD.4	Generate measurement data by measuring lengths using rulers marked with halves and fourths of an inch. Show the data by making a line plot, where the horizontal scale is marked off in appropriate units—whole numbers, halves, or quarters.	Unit 3 Lessons 1, 13, 14, 15

Geometric measurement: understand concepts of area and relate area to multiplication and to addition.

3.MD.5	Recognize area as an attribute of plane figures and understand concepts of area measurement.	Unit 1 Lesson 11; Unit 2 Lesson 2; Unit 6 Lessons 5, 7
3.MD.5a	A square with side length 1 unit, called "a unit square," is said to have "one square unit" of area, and can be used to measure area.	Unit 1 Lesson 11; Unit 2 Lesson 2; Unit 6 Lessons 5, 7
3.MD.5b	A plane figure that can be covered without gaps or overlaps by n unit squares is said to have an area of n square units.	Unit 1 Lesson 11; Unit 2 Lesson 2; Unit 6 Lessons 5, 7

3.MD.6	Measure areas by counting unit squares (square cm, square m, square in, square ft, and improvised units).	Unit 1 Lesson 11; Unit 6 Lessons 5, 6, 10
3.MD.7	Relate area to the operations of multiplication and addition.	Unit 1 Lesson 11, 12, 14; Unit 2 Lessons 2, 6, 8; Unit 6 Lessons 5, 6, 7, 8, 9,11
3.MD.7a	Find the area of a rectangle with whole-number side lengths by tiling it, and show that the area is the same as would be found by multiplying the side lengths.	Unit 1 Lesson 11; Unit 2 Lesson 2; Unit 6 Lessons 5, 6
3.MD.7b	Multiply side lengths to find areas of rectangles with whole number side lengths in the context of solving real world and mathematical problems, and represent whole-number products as rectangular areas in mathematical reasoning.	Unit 1 Lessons 11, 12, 14; Unit 2 Lessons 2, 6; Unit 6 Lessons 5, 6, 7, 8, 9
3.MD.7c	Use tiling to show in a concrete case that the area of a rectangle with whole-number side lengths a and $b + c$ is the sum of $a \times b$ and $a \times c$. Use area models to represent the distributive property in mathematical reasoning.	Unit 1 Lessons 11, 12, 14; Unit 6 Lesson 6
3.MD.7d	Recognize area as additive. Find areas of rectilinear figures by decomposing them into non-overlapping rectangles and adding the areas of the non-overlapping parts, applying this technique to solve real world problems.	Unit 1 Lesson 11; Unit 2 Lessons 2, 6, 8; Unit 6 Lessons 6, 8, 9, 11

Geometric measurement: recognize perimeter as an attribute of plane figures and distinguish between linear and area measures.

3.MD.8	Solve real world and mathematical problems involving perimeters of polygons, including finding the perimeter given the side lengths, finding an unknown side length, and exhibiting rectangles with the same perimeter and different areas or with the same area and different perimeters.	Unit 6 Lessons 5, 6, 7, 9, 11

3.G Geometry

Reason with shapes and their attributes.

CC.3.G.1	Understand that shapes in different categories (e.g., rhombuses, rectangles, and others) may share attributes (e.g., having four sides), and that the shared attributes can define a larger category (e.g., quadrilaterals). Recognize rhombuses, rectangles, and squares as examples of quadrilaterals, and draw examples of quadrilaterals that do not belong to any of these subcategories.	Unit 6 Lessons 1, 2, 3, 4, 11
CC.3.G.2	Partition shapes into parts with equal areas. Express the area of each part as a unit fraction of the whole.	Unit 6 Lesson 1; Unit 7 Lessons 1, 2, 9

California Common Core Standards for Mathematical Practice

MP.1 Make sense of problems and persevere in solving them.

Mathematically proficient students start by explaining to themselves the meaning of a problem and looking for entry points to its solution. They analyze givens, constraints, relationships, and goals. They make conjectures about the form and meaning of the solution and plan a solution pathway rather than simply jumping into a solution attempt. They consider analogous problems, and try special cases and simpler forms of the original problem in order to gain insight into its solution. They monitor and evaluate their progress and change course if necessary. Older students might, depending on the context of the problem, transform algebraic expressions or change the viewing window on their graphing calculator to get the information they need. Mathematically proficient students can explain correspondences between equations, verbal descriptions, tables, and graphs or draw diagrams of important features and relationships, graph data, and search for regularity or trends. Younger students might rely on using concrete objects or pictures to help conceptualize and solve a problem. Mathematically proficient students check their answers to problems using a different method, and they continually ask themselves, "Does this make sense?" They can understand the approaches of others to solving complex problems and identify correspondences between different approaches.

Unit 1 Lessons 3, 4, 5, 6, 7, 9, 10, 12, 13, 14, 16, 18, 19

Unit 2 Lessons 1, 2, 4, 7, 9, 10, 11, 13, 15

Unit 3 Lessons 2, 3, 4, 5, 6, 8, 9, 10, 11, 12, 13, 14, 15

Unit 4 Lessons 3, 4, 5, 6, 7, 8, 9, 10, 11, 12, 13, 14, 15, 16, 17, 18

Unit 5 Lessons 1, 2, 3, 4, 6, 7, 8, 9, 10, 11

Unit 6 Lessons 6, 9, 11

Unit 7 Lessons 2, 3, 7, 8, 9

MP.2 Reason abstractly and quantitatively.

Mathematically proficient students make sense of quantities and their relationships in problem situations. They bring two complementary abilities to bear on problems involving quantitative relationships: the ability to *decontextualize*—to abstract a given situation and represent it symbolically and manipulate the representing symbols as if they have a life of their own, without necessarily attending to their referents—and the ability to *contextualize*, to pause as needed during the manipulation process in order to probe into the referents for the symbols involved. Quantitative reasoning entails habits of creating a coherent representation of the problem at hand; considering the units involved; attending to the meaning of quantities, not just how to compute them; and knowing and flexibly using different properties of operations and objects.

Unit 1 Lessons 1, 2, 3, 5, 6, 7, 8, 10, 11, 12, 19

Unit 2 Lessons 1, 2, 3, 5, 6, 8, 13, 15

Unit 3 Lessons 1, 2, 3, 4, 8, 12, 13, 15

Unit 4 Lessons 1, 2, 5, 6, 9, 11, 12, 13, 14, 15, 16, 17, 18

Unit 5 Lessons 1, 2, 3, 4, 8, 11

Unit 6 Lessons 1, 5, 6, 7, 8, 9, 11

Unit 7 Lessons 1, 2, 3, 4, 5, 6, 7, 8, 9

MP.3 Construct viable arguments and critique the reasoning of others.

Mathematically proficient students understand and use stated assumptions, definitions, and previously established results in constructing arguments. They make conjectures and build a logical progression of statements to explore the truth of their conjectures. They are able to analyze situations by breaking them into cases, and can recognize and use counterexamples. They justify their conclusions, communicate them to others, and respond to the arguments of others. They reason inductively about data, making plausible arguments that take into account the context from which the data arose. Mathematically proficient students are also able to compare the effectiveness of two plausible arguments, distinguish correct logic or reasoning from that which is flawed, and—if there is a flaw in an argument—explain what it is. Elementary students can construct arguments using concrete referents such as objects, drawings, diagrams, and actions. Such arguments can make sense and be correct, even though they are not generalized or made formal until later grades. Later, students learn to determine domains to which an argument applies. Students at all grades can listen or read the arguments of others, decide whether they make sense, and ask useful questions to clarify or improve the arguments.

Unit 1 Lessons 1, 2, 3, 4, 5, 6, 7, 8, 9, 10, 11, 12, 13, 14, 15, 16, 18, 19

Unit 2 Lessons 1, 2, 3, 4, 5, 6, 8, 9, 10, 11, 12, 13, 14, 15

Unit 3 Lessons 1, 2, 3, 4, 5, 6, 7, 8, 9, 10, 12, 13, 14, 15

Unit 4 Lessons 1, 2, 3, 4, 5, 6, 7, 8, 9, 10, 11, 12, 13, 14, 15, 16, 17, 18

Unit 5 Lessons 1, 2, 3, 4, 5, 6, 7, 8, 9, 10, 11

Unit 6 Lessons 1, 2, 3, 4, 5, 6, 7, 8, 9, 10, 11

Unit 7 Lessons 1, 2, 3, 4, 5, 6, 7, 8, 9

MP.4 Model with mathematics.

Mathematically proficient students can apply the mathematics they know to solve problems arising in everyday life, society, and the workplace. In early grades, this might be as simple as writing an addition equation to describe a situation. In middle grades, a student might apply proportional reasoning to plan a school event or analyze a problem in the community. By high school, a student might use geometry to solve a design problem or use a function to describe how one quantity of interest depends on another. Mathematically proficient students who can apply what they know are comfortable making assumptions and approximations to simplify a complicated situation, realizing that these may need revision later. They are able to identify important quantities in a practical situation and map their relationships using such tools as diagrams, two-way tables, graphs, flowcharts and formulas. They can analyze those relationships mathematically to draw conclusions. They routinely interpret their mathematical results in the context of the situation and reflect on whether the results make sense, possibly improving the model if it has not served its purpose.

Unit 1 Lessons 1, 2, 3, 4, 5, 6, 7, 8, 9, 10, 12, 13, 14, 16, 18, 19

Unit 2 Lessons 2, 4, 7, 9, 11, 13, 15

Unit 3 Lessons 2, 3, 4, 5, 6, 8, 9, 10, 11, 12, 13, 15

Unit 4 Lessons 3, 4, 7, 8, 9, 10, 11, 12, 14, 17, 18

Unit 5 Lessons 1, 2, 3, 4, 8, 9, 10, 11

Unit 6 Lessons 6, 9, 10, 11

Unit 7 Lessons 3, 8, 9

MP.5 Use appropriate tools strategically.

Mathematically proficient students consider the available tools when solving a mathematical problem. These tools might include pencil and paper, concrete models, a ruler, a protractor, a calculator, a spreadsheet, a computer algebra system, a statistical package, or dynamic geometry software. Proficient students are sufficiently familiar with tools appropriate for their grade or course to make sound decisions about when each of these tools might be helpful, recognizing both the insight to be gained and their limitations. For example, mathematically proficient high school students analyze graphs of functions and solutions generated using a graphing calculator. They detect possible errors by strategically using estimation and other mathematical knowledge. When making mathematical models, they know that technology can enable them to visualize the results of varying assumptions, explore consequences, and compare predictions with data. Mathematically proficient students at various grade levels are able to identify relevant external mathematical resources, such as digital content located on a website, and use them to pose or solve problems. They are able to use technological tools to explore and deepen their understanding of concepts.

Unit 1 Lessons 1, 2, 3, 4, 5, 6, 7, 8, 9, 10, 11, 12, 13, 14, 15, 16, 17, 18, 19

Unit 2 Lessons 1, 2, 3, 4, 5, 6, 7, 8, 9, 10, 11, 12, 13, 14, 15

Unit 3 Lessons 1, 2, 3, 4, 6, 7, 8, 9, 10, 13, 15

Unit 4 Lessons 1, 2, 3, 4, 5, 6, 7, 8, 13, 17, 18

Unit 5 Lessons 1, 2, 3, 4, 11

Unit 6 Lessons 1, 3, 4, 5, 6, 10, 11

Unit 7 Lessons 1, 2, 3, 5, 6, 7, 9

MP.6 Attend to precision.

Mathematically proficient students try to communicate precisely to others. They try to use clear definitions in discussion with others and in their own reasoning. They state the meaning of the symbols they choose, including using the equal sign consistently and appropriately. They are careful about specifying units of measure, and labeling axes to clarify the correspondence with quantities in a problem. They calculate accurately and efficiently, express numerical answers with a degree of precision appropriate for the problem context. In the elementary grades, students give carefully formulated explanations to each other. By the time they reach high school they have learned to examine claims and make explicit use of definitions.

Unit 1 Lessons 1, 2, 3, 4, 5, 6, 7, 8, 9, 10, 11, 12, 13, 14, 15, 16, 18, 19

Unit 2 Lessons 1, 2, 3, 4, 5, 6, 7, 8, 9, 10, 11, 12, 13, 14, 15

Unit 3 Lessons 1, 2, 3, 4, 5, 6, 7, 8, 9, 10, 11, 12, 13, 14, 15

Unit 4 Lessons 1, 2, 3, 4, 5, 6, 7, 8, 9, 10, 11, 12, 13, 14, 15, 16, 17, 18

Unit 5 Lessons 1, 2, 3, 4, 5, 6, 7, 8, 9, 10, 11

Unit 6 Lessons 1, 2, 3, 4, 5, 6, 7, 8, 9, 10, 11

Unit 7 Lessons 1, 2, 3, 4, 5, 6, 7, 8, 9

MP.7 Look for and make use of structure.

Mathematically proficient students look closely to discern a pattern or structure. Young students, for example, might notice that three and seven more is the same amount as seven and three more, or they may sort a collection of shapes according to how many sides the shapes have. Later, students will see 7×8 equals the well remembered $7 \times 5 + 7 \times 3$, in preparation for learning about the distributive property. In the expression $x^2 + 9x + 14$, older students can see the 14 as 2×7 and the 9 as $2 + 7$. They recognize the significance of an existing line in a geometric figure and can use the strategy of drawing an auxiliary line for solving problems. They also can step back for an overview and shift perspective. They can see complicated things, such as some algebraic expressions, as single objects or as being composed of several objects. For example, they can see $5 - 3(x - y)^2$ as 5 minus a positive number times a square and use that to realize that its value cannot be more than 5 for any real numbers x and y.

Unit 1 Lessons 1, 2, 4, 5, 6, 7, 8, 10, 11, 12, 13, 15, 19

Unit 2 Lessons 1, 3, 5, 6, 14, 15

Unit 3 Lessons 2, 15

Unit 4 Lessons 1, 2, 3, 4, 11, 14, 16, 17, 18

Unit 5 Lessons 1, 2, 3, 4, 5, 8, 11

Unit 6 Lessons 1, 2, 3, 4, 5, 8, 10, 11

Unit 7 Lessons 1, 2, 3, 6, 9

MP.8 Look for and express regularity in repeated reasoning.

Mathematically proficient students notice if calculations are repeated, and look both for general methods and for shortcuts. Upper elementary students might notice when dividing 25 by 11 that they are repeating the same calculations over and over again, and conclude they have a repeating decimal. By paying attention to the calculation of slope as they repeatedly check whether points are on the line through (1, 2) with slope 3, middle school students might abstract the equation $(y - 2)/(x - 1) = 3$. Noticing the regularity in the way terms cancel when expanding $(x - 1)(x + 1)$, $(x - 1)$ $(x^2 + x + 1)$, and $(x - 1)(x^3 + x^2 + x + 1)$ might lead them to the general formula for the sum of a geometric series. As they work to solve a problem, mathematically proficient students maintain oversight of the process, while attending to the details. They continually evaluate the reasonableness of their intermediate results.

Unit 1 Lessons 1, 2, 3, 5, 7, 8, 10, 11, 12, 19

Unit 2 Lessons 1, 2, 3, 5, 6, 10, 12, 14, 15

Unit 3 Lessons 1, 14, 15

Unit 4 Lessons 5, 6, 14, 17, 18

Unit 5 Lessons 1, 4, 9, 11

Unit 6 Lessons 4, 7, 10, 11

Unit 7 Lessons 1, 2, 3, 5, 6, 9

Index

B

C

more or fewer, 289–290

unknown amount, 287

use comparison bars, 286–288

using data in a bar graph, 206

using data in a pictograph, 205

Computational algorithms, methods, and strategies. *See* **Addition; Subtraction**

Content Overview

Unit 1, 1–4, 11–14

Unit 2, 93–94

Unit 3, 165–166, 185–186, 199–200

Unit 4, 223–226

Unit 5, 271–272

Unit 6, 313–314, 333–334

Unit 7, 367–368

Count-bys

0s and 1s, 49

2s, 17

3s, 49

4s, 49

5s, 17

6s, 97

7s, 97

8s, 97

9s, 17

10s, 17

squares, 97

Customary Units of Measurement

capacity, 171–174

length, 167–170

weight, 177–178

D

Dash Record Sheet, 16

Dashes, 77–82, 125–130, 143–148

Data

analyze

from a bar graph, 206, 207–208, 210, 213

from a frequency table, 211, 212, 216

from a pictograph, 86, 158, 201, 205

from a table, 158, 306

from a tally chart, 212

compare

from a frequency table, 212

from a line plot, 211

from a pictograph, 86, 201, 205

from a table, 204, 211

from a tally chart, 211

display

using a bar graph, 206–208

using a line plot, 211–212

using a pictograph, 86, 158

using a table, 204, 211

using a tally chart, 212

organize

using a bar graph, 204, 209–210

using a frequency table, 211, 216

using a line plot, 212, 214

using a pictograph, 86, 158, 202

using a tally chart, 212, 216

Decompose Figures

two-dimensional figures, 51–52, 56–57, 339–340, 345–348

Distributive Property, 51–52, 56–57, 63, 339–340

Dividend, 23

zero as, 66

Division, 23–26

0s, 65–71

1s, 65–71

2s, 27–32

3s, 45–48

4s, 49–55

E

© Houghton Mifflin Harcourt Publishing Company

Expression, 276

evaluate by using order of operations, 135–136

F

Factor, 6, 279–280, 283–284. *See also*
Multiplication, by

0,1,2,3,4,5,6,7,8,9,10

Family Letter, 1–4, 11–14, 93–94, 165–166, 185–186, 199–200, 223–226, 271–272, 313–314, 333–334, 367–368

Fast array drawings, 44, 106, 112

Focus on Mathematical Practices, 85–86, 157–158, 215–216, 263–264, 305–306, 359–360, 389–390

Fraction circles, to model fractions as parts of a whole, 381–381A

Fraction rectangles, to model fractions as parts of a whole, 369A–369B

Fractions, 169, 212, 373, 387–388

compare, 379–380, 381–382

denominator, 371

equivalence chains, 383, 385–386

equivalent, 383A–386

express as whole numbers, 376–378

locate on a number line, 375–378

numerator, 371

on a number line, 374–378, 380, 385–386, 387–388

part of a whole, 369A–371, 381–381A

unit, 369–372, 379–380

Fraction bars, 371, 373, 379

Fraction strips

to model equivalent fractions, 383A–384

Frequency tables, 204, 209, 211, 212, 216

Functions

finding and writing the rule, 10

function table, 10

using a rule, 10

G

Geometry, 315

adjacent sides, 326

angle, 315, 316, 318

concave, 319

convex, 319

decagon, 320–321A

hexagon, 320–321A

octagon, 320–321A

opposite sides, 324

parallelogram, 321–322, 325–332

pentagon, 320–321A

polygon, 319

quadrilateral, 319A, 323–332, 333A

ray, 315

rectangle, 322, 323, 326, 329–332, 343–344, 369A–370

rhombus, 322, 327, 329–330, 332

right angle, 315

square, 322, 327, 329, 330, 332

tangram pieces, 353A–358

trapezoid, 324, 332

triangle, 370

acute, 316

classifying, 316–319A

isosceles, 317

obtuse, 316

right, 316

two-dimensional figures, 353A–358

decompose, 345–348

polygons, 319A–321A

Glossary, S13

Index (continued)

Graphs

bar, 203–204, 206, 207–210, 213
frequency tables, 204, 211–212, 216
line plot, 212, 214
pictograph, 28, 86, 158, 201–202, 205

Grouping

in addition, 240, 243

H

Hexagons, 320

I

Identity Property

of addition, 67
of multiplication, 67

Inequality, 276, 285

L

Length

customary units, 167–170
estimate, 168

Line plot, 169–170

generate data with halves and fourths, 168, 170, 212, 216
making, 170, 212, 216
reading and interpreting, 211, 214

Line segment, 167

Liquid Volume (Capacity), 183

customary units, 171–174
estimate, 172–175
metric units, 175–176
using drawings, 173–176

M

Manipulatives

base ten blocks, 141
Check Sheets
0s-10s, 118
1s and 0s, 71–72
2s, 5s, 9s, and 10s, 41–42
3s and 4s, 53–54
5s and 2s, 29–30
6s, 7s, and 8s, 117
6s and 8s, 103–104
7s and squares, 113–114
10s and 9s, 37–38
clocks (analog), 187A-187B
Dashes, 77–82, 125–130, 143–148
Dash Record Sheet, 15
Division Race Game Board, 75
fraction circles, 381–381B
fraction rectangles, 369A–369B
fraction strips, 383A–384
multiplication tables (Targets), 31
Number Path, 45, 111
Paper Clock, 187A–187B
perimeter and area, 337A–337B
Product Cards, 153A–153J
Quadrilaterals for sorting, 333A–333B
rulers, 167–168, 360
Secret Code Cards, 229A–229D
Signature Sheet, 15
Strategy Cards, 51A–51Z
Study Sheets, 17–18, 49–50, 97–98
tangrams, 353A–358
Targets, 31
Three-in-a-Row Game Grids, 75, 152
triangles to build quadrilaterals and polygons, 319A–319B, 321A–321B

Mass, 179–182, 184

  estimate, 182

  units of, 179

Math Mountain, 273–275

  relate addition and subtraction, 256, 259, 278

  total, 282

  unknown number, 281–282

Math Talk

  In Activities, 55, 85, 156, 172, 182, 183, 208, 211, 214, 215, 247, 276, 282, 305, 318, 319, 321, 324, 329, 332, 343, 344, 354, 359

  Math Talk in Action, 34, 52, 55, 58, 111, 137, 171, 197, 204, 213, 234, 263, 331, 335, 352

Measurement. *See also* **Estimate; Time**

  area

    on a dot array, 335–336

    of a rectangle, 100–102, 336–348, 369A–370

    of a square, 336

    square units, 19, 100, 335–338

    word problems, 172–184, 349–352

  centimeter, 335, 336

  generate data for line plots, 168, 170, 212, 216

  inch, 167, 168

  length

    customary units, 167–170

    estimate, 168

  liquid volume (capacity), 183

    customary units, 171–174

    estimate, 172–175

    measure, 171–174

    metric units, 175–176

    using drawings, 173–176

  mass, 178–182, 184

    benchmarks, 179

    estimate, 182

    using drawings, 177–180

  perimeter, 335–336

    on a dot array, 335–336

    of a rectangle or square, 335–336, 339–344

    word problems, 349–352

    problem solving, 173–174, 176, 178, 180, 183–184, 197–198, 349–352

  time

    add, 195

    before and after the hour, 187, 188, 191–192

    A.M. and P.M., 188, 193, 194, 197–198

    analog clock, 187, 188, 189, 190–193, 197–198

    digital clock, 187, 188, 189, 190

    elapsed time, 193–194

    subtract, 196

  to the minute, 190–192

  to five minutes, 191

  using a clock to find, 187, 188, 189, 190–194, 197–198

  using a number line diagram to find, 195–198

  weight

    customary units, 177–178

    estimate, 182

Mental math

  multiplication, 142

Missing addend. *See* **Algebra**

Multiplication

  by 0, 65–71

  by 1, 65–71

  by 2, 27–32

  by 3, 45–48

  by 4, 55–58

  by 5, 5–10, 17–23, 29–32

  by 6, 95–98

N

O

P

Patterns

count-bys and multiplication, 27, 31, 33, 40, 45, 55, 95, 105, 111, 155–156

on a multiplication table, 31, 116, 155–156

square numbers, 115–116

Pentagons, 320

Perimeter, 335–336

find unknown side lengths, 341–342

on a dot array, 335–336

of a rectangle or square, 335–336, 341–344

rectangles with same area and different perimeter, 344

rectangles with same perimeter and different area, 343

word problems, 349–352

Pictograph, 201

key, 201

making, 202

reading and interpreting, 28, 86, 158, 201, 202, 205

problem solving with, 28, 86, 158, 201, 202, 205

Place value, 227, 231

to add and subtract multidigit numbers, 239–242, 247

to round, 235

through hundreds, 227

through thousands, 228

in word problems, 230, 236, 241

Place value drawings, 227–228, 230, 247

circles, 227, 228

hundred-box, 227, 249–250

ten-stick, 227

thousand-bar, 228

Plane figures. *See* **Geometry, two-dimensional figures**

Problem Solving

problem types

addition and subtraction, 234, 245–246, 257–258

area and/or perimeter, 100–102, 336–338, 341–344, 349–352

array, 21

comparison, 286–290

extra, hidden, or not enough information, 291–292

fractions, 387–388

hidden information, 292

liquid volume (capacity), 173–176, 183

multiplication and division, 21, 28, 32, 34, 35, 43, 121–122

not enough information, 293–294

Put Together/Take Apart, 275

relate addition and subtraction, 255–256

Too Much or Not Enough Information, 291, 293–294

Two-Step, 137–139, 149, 295–296, 301–304

Unknown Start, 281–282

weight, 178

skills

choose the operation, 107, 131–132

use a graph, 201–203, 205–208, 210, 213–214

use Associative and Commutative Properties to solve, 66, 67

write the question, 133, 137–138, 295–296

write word problems, 32, 64, 70, 84, 122, 134

strategies

Comparison Bars, 286–288

Draw a Picture, 21, 101, 102

Proof Drawings, 239–241, 249–251, 255

Product, 6

Proof Drawings

for addition, 239–241, 255

for subtraction, 249–251

Properties

Associative

of addition, 66, 67

of multiplication, 66, 141

Commutative

of multiplication, 22, 67, 141

Distributive, 51–52, 56–57, 63, 337–340

Identity

of addition, 67

of multiplication, 67

Zero, 66, 67

Puzzled Penguin, 25, 36, 58, 109, 136, 171, 181, 198, 238, 242, 248, 289, 297, 331, 348, 382, 384

Q

Quadrilateral, 319A, 323–324, 329–332, 333A

draw, 325–328

parallelogram, 321–322, 325–332

rectangle, 322, 323, 326, 329–332, 343–344, 369A–370

rhombus, 322, 327, 329, 332

square, 327, 329, 330, 332

trapezoid, 323–324

Quotient, 23

R

Real world problems. *See* **Problem Solving, problem types**

Reasonable answers, 234, 237, 262, 299–300

Rectangle, 322, 323, 326, 329–332, 343–344, 369A

Rhombus, 322, 327, 329, 332

Round, 233, 235–236, 237–238

to estimate differences, 234, 237

to estimate sums, 234, 237, 245–246, 299

rules, 233, 235

S

Secret Code Cards, 229A–229D

Show All Totals method, 239

Signature Sheet, 15

Square, 322, 327, 329, 331, 332

Square Numbers, 115–116

Standard form, 229

Strategies for Adding and Subtracting, 239, 240, 241–242, 273–275

use properties, 67

use relationship between addition and subtraction, 255–256

Strategies for Multiplying and Dividing, 63, 96, 102, 106, 133

patterns, 27, 31, 40, 45, 55

use a known fact to find an unknown one, 26

use properties, 66–68, 153

use relationship between multiplication and division, 24, 26, 34

use shortcuts, 46–47, 56, 141

Strategy Cards, 51A–51Z

Study Sheets, 17–18, 49–50, 97–98

Subtraction, 248, 254

across zeros, 249–252

equations, 276

T

U

V

Multiplication Table and Scrambled Tables (Volume 2)

E

×	4	2	5	1	3	8	10	7	9	6
4	16	8	20	4	12	32	40	28	36	24
1	4	2	5	1	3	8	10	7	9	6
2	8	4	10	2	6	16	20	14	18	12
5	20	10	25	5	15	40	50	35	45	30
3	12	6	15	3	9	24	30	21	27	18
9	36	18	45	9	27	72	90	63	81	54
6	24	12	30	6	18	48	60	42	54	36
10	40	20	50	10	30	80	100	70	90	60
7	28	14	35	7	21	56	70	49	63	42
8	32	16	40	8	24	64	80	56	72	48

F

×	9	8	6	7	4	6	8	7	4	9
2	18	16	12	14	8	12	16	14	8	18
3	27	24	18	21	12	18	24	21	12	27
5	45	40	30	35	20	30	40	35	20	45
3	27	24	18	21	12	18	24	21	12	27
5	45	40	30	35	20	30	40	35	20	45
9	81	72	54	63	36	54	72	63	36	81
7	63	56	42	49	28	42	56	49	28	63
6	54	48	36	42	24	36	48	42	24	54
8	72	64	48	56	32	48	64	56	32	72
4	36	32	24	28	16	24	32	28	16	36

G

×	7	6	8	7	8	6	8	7	6	8
5	35	30	40	35	40	30	40	35	30	40
4	28	24	32	28	32	24	32	28	24	32
3	21	18	24	21	24	18	24	21	18	24
2	14	12	16	14	16	12	16	14	12	16
8	56	48	64	56	64	48	64	56	48	64
9	63	54	72	63	72	54	72	63	54	72
7	49	42	56	49	56	42	56	49	42	56
6	42	36	48	42	48	36	48	42	36	48
8	56	48	64	56	64	48	64	56	48	64
6	42	36	48	42	48	36	48	42	36	48

H

×	4	6	7	8	9	6	9	8	7	4
4	16	24	28	32	36	24	36	32	28	16
6	24	36	42	48	54	36	54	48	42	24
7	28	42	49	56	63	42	63	56	49	28
8	32	48	56	64	72	48	72	64	56	32
9	36	54	63	72	81	54	81	72	63	36
8	32	48	56	64	72	48	72	64	56	32
9	36	54	63	72	81	54	81	72	63	36
4	16	24	28	32	36	24	36	32	28	16
7	28	42	49	56	63	42	63	56	49	28
6	24	36	42	48	54	36	54	48	42	24